Teacher Research

Teacher Research
From Promise to Power

Leslie Patterson
John C. Stansell
Sharon Lee

with contributions by
R. Kay Moss and Terresa Payne Katt

RICHARD C. OWEN PUBLISHERS, INC.
Katonah, New York

Library of Congress Cataloging-in-Publication Data
Patterson, Leslie.
   Teacher research : from promise to power / Leslie Patterson, John C.
Stansell, Sharon Lee, with contributions by R. Kay Moss, Terresa
Payne Katt.
      p.   cm.
   Includes bibliographical references and index.
   ISBN 1-878450-09-3
   1. Language arts—Evaluation.   2. Education—Research—
Methodology.   I. Stansell, John C.   II. Lee, Sharon, 1955–
III. Title.
LB1576.P275   1990
370'.7'8—dc20   90-36504
                                                          CIP

RICHARD C. OWEN PUBLISHERS, INC.
135 Katonah Avenue
Katonah, New York 10536

Printed in the United States of America
Cover design by Kenneth J. Hawkey

Contents

Preface

"Kidwatching" has become a way of life for many language arts teachers. The informal assessment and the theory-based instructional decision making that Yetta Goodman advocated when she first introduced the term more than ten years ago is now commonplace, especially among whole language teachers. In this book we argue that teachers can move beyond kidwatching to do systematic research in their classrooms. We argue that teachers' research can inform specific instructional decisions, but we also explore the potential for these research findings to influence teachers' personal theories and our collective theoretical understandings. Teacher research promises to offer teachers a tool for professional development and a vehicle for gaining power in the profession and in policy-making arenas.

This book is not intended to be an exhaustive review of every issue which might be important to teacher researchers, and it does not argue that teacher research is the answer to all our problems. For example, we do not propose that teachers should be the *only* researchers in education. Sociologists, linguists, psychologists, anthropologists, and others make unique and vital contributions to our knowledge of how human beings learn. But we do think that teachers can take every opportunity to learn from those research traditions and that they are fully capable of joining those researchers as peers.

This book will not train teachers to do research. Although we recognize the value of research training, teachers do not have to complete a training program before attempting a first project. We learn to write by writing; we learn to read by reading; and we learn to research by doing research. We have tried to suggest some design possibilities and methodological alternatives, but we urge readers to view them only as starting points.

Besides, becoming a topnotch researcher is more than mastering a given set of techniques; it also involves years of developing a way of looking at the world and inventing ways of asking questions about it.

We do not ignore the institutional constraints on teachers who want to do research, but we regard them as temporary. We recognize that those constraints are resistant to change, yet we have seen many individual teachers who don't accept the old but-they-won't-let-us-do-it argument. We are convinced that in time the profession can change existing policies and practices to support teachers who want to do research.

This book also does not address the potential for teacher research across disciplines. Our backgrounds are in language, literature, and literacy, and the teachers we describe are language arts teachers, although most of what we will say can be applied to any classroom, any teaching/learning context. We invite you to make those connections as you read.

Finally, although this book presents a naturalistic approach to research we have chosen not to include an extensive explanation or defense of that research paradigm or framework. We believe that the most powerful data about instruction come from authentic learning situations in real classrooms. That calls for systematic observation, interviews, document analysis, and other naturalistic methodologies like those used by Lucy Calkins, Nancie Atwell, Donald Graves, Janet Emig, and others. We respect different research traditions and suggest that teachers choose an approach to research that is consistent with their philosophical and theoretical positions toward teaching and learning.

The first part of the book focuses on the *process* of teacher research—first, an invitation to do research as a classroom teacher followed by a discussion of how questions can lead to decisions about data-gathering and data analysis (Chapter 2). Then a teacher researcher gives her account of how her questions led to the research process, which leads to further questions, and so on (Chapter 3).

The second part focuses on the *products* of teacher research. First, we discuss how teacher research helps build theory (Chapter 4), followed by a teacher researcher's account of her personal theory-building process (Chapter 5).

In the next part, the sixth chapter, written by Kay Moss, provides an important resource for teachers who want to share the products of their classroom studies. Terresa Payne Katt contributes (Chapter 7) an illustration of how the presentation of research findings helped her gain credibility and prominence within her district and beyond.

The final part deals with *power*, exploring how classroom studies can help teachers who do research in their quests to take control of their professional lives (Chapter 8). Questions which initiated the research process now sustain the quest.

Together the three of us have spent the last eight years or so asking questions about philosophy, theory, kids, teachers, and research. Maybe John started our quest when, in his role as advisor and mentor in the Texas A & M University doctoral program, he expected his students to ask questions. Leslie and Sharon entered that program at about the same time and were asking similar types of questions. Now John is working with new doctoral students, and Leslie and Sharon are at other universities, teaching and learning with their own students. Leslie is at Sam Houston State University, Huntsville, Texas, and Sharon is at the University of South Dakota in Vermillion. All of us are continuing to urge teachers and preservice teachers to become close observers and researchers, as well as trying to make time to do research in our classes.

In recent years our circle of teacher researcher colleagues has grown. We have had opportunities to learn from many classroom researchers. We have watched those teachers making significant changes on their campuses and beyond. We have also come to know colleagues across the country who are involved with similar questions, similar quests. We suspect that our voices may echo what is happening in many schools and universities across the United States. We hope that this book will help you and your colleagues ask your own questions.

This book can be used in several ways—by sharing it with a support group, as part of a graduate course or staff development workshop, or on your own. However you read it we encourage you to join with at least one colleague and explore classroom research together. Investigate the questions that bother you, the puzzles you see.

Now, let's get started on Chapter 1.

—L.P.
J.C.S.
S.L.

Acknowledgments

This book is the result of a collaborative effort over several years, and it isn't possible to list all the people who have contributed to our thinking about teachers and research. Only some of their names are mentioned in the book. We know some of them only through their writing and conference presentations. We have met others in workshops and graduate classes. Still others are researching teachers who have generously shared their work with us. We sincerely thank each one of them.

Specific thanks go to our friends and colleagues who read drafts of the manuscript and offered thoughtful and honest critiques: Ruth Holladay, E. Bess Osburn, Joan Prouty, Zoa Ragsdale, and Philip Swicegood; and to our reviewers: Nancy Andrews, Jane White, and Ann Ziegler. Thanks also to Richard C. Owen for his confidence and patience throughout the writing and publishing process, and to Louise Waller for her editorial expertise.

Finally, a special thank you to our families for continuing to show their support in ways that no others can.

1. Teachers, Questions, and Quests: An Invitation to Classroom Research

There were seven of them sitting around the table—six secondary-school language arts teachers and Leslie Patterson, a newly appointed university professor. The teachers had signed up to take a course in research and Leslie, who had recently left her position as a high-school teacher researcher, was there to demonstrate options and to respond to questions. Betty Higgins, who had already completed two classroom research projects, said, "I'm warning you. After this semester you'll be hooked. You'll never again be able to teach without some kind of research question in mind." She went on to say that after doing research she would never again look at her students in quite the same way. Before she had looked out from her desk at a group of faces; now she saw individuals. Before she had graded and recorded scores in her gradebook; now she saw those writing products as evidence of individual growth.

During that semester not all six teachers felt the same "hook" that Higgins had, but all of them insisted that the research they carried out changed their teaching in some significant way.

Lucy Calkins, in *The Art of Teaching Writing* (1986), eloquently convinces the reader that all children have stories to tell. She convinces us that the teacher's job is to enfranchise all students, to help them find their voices and respond to their unique and powerful stories. We believe that; and we believe the same thing about teachers and research.

Every teacher has stories to tell. Every teacher has truths to share. Teachers can learn to see children in ways that no one else can. Teachers can show us the ways their students learn, and the reasons that learning is sometimes hard. The research process can help teachers explore their decisions, find their own voices, and tell their own stories. Through those stories that are based on disciplined, systematic research many teachers have spoken out and changed the ways in which schools work. Ultimately, through research, all teachers can do this—and that is an exciting prospect. When schools depend more on the leadership of teachers who do research and control their own professional lives, there will be no need for prepackaged curricula that treat both teachers and children as incapable. Then, the real capabilities of both groups of learners can be seen, appreciated, and developed.

Teachers are beginning to take control of their professional lives. The whole language movement around the world reflects this trend. As whole language teachers continue to learn from one another and from their students, they expand and assert their own expertise and grow less and less willing to accept the dictates of textbook publishers, legislators, and administrators. Committed to an explicit theory base, these teachers make individual instructional decisions in response to their students' needs— individual decisions that, collectively, offer increasingly attractive alternatives to a curriculum dominated by basal publishers, external curriculum developers, and test-makers. They have begun to replace basals with real literature, to provide authentic reading and writing experiences for students, to develop new assessment and evaluation procedures, and to organize support groups like Teachers Applying Whole Language (TAWL) that allow them to develop and share their expertise.

Like other teachers who are taking control, whole language teachers see themselves as learners and teaching as a learning process. For many of them classroom research is becoming a critical aspect of their teaching. Many of these teachers are already conducting research in their classrooms. Others are interested in finding out what classroom research involves and how they might try it. As more and more teachers use research to learn from their students, we see more and more diversity in research paradigms, the research process, and in the resulting products.

For example, some teacher researchers use quasi-experimental designs to test instructional approaches and interventions, drawing on the more familiar paradigm of educational research. Other teacher researchers share classroom experiences with colleagues in order to solve specific curricular problems. Still others adopt the stance and methodology of anthropologists as they observe, question, and look for patterns in a natural setting.

Some researchers work alone. Others work with colleagues across the hall or across the district. Still others work with university researchers in a variety of collaborative arrangements. We see this diversity as a healthy growth sign and an indication of wide interest.

This diversity exists because people view the world differently. The view of teacher research that you will see in this book is a reflection of our particular view of the world, so it may differ from other descriptions of teacher research that you have heard. Central to our view is the notion that teaching, learning, and researching are all ongoing, transactional processes through which we are constantly changing. What this book provides is not a definitive explanation of teacher research but simply what we are currently thinking. We offer the book as a springboard to further discussion and exploration.

I
PROCESS

2. Any Questions? Find the Answers in Your Classroom!

So how do we get started? Maybe the best approach to that question is an indirect one that connects the familiar process of looking at things carefully with the process of teacher research.

Imagine a landscape photographer hired to take pictures of a national park for a travel magazine. The photographer wants to capture some specific features of the area that make it unique and appealing to travelers. As she unloads her equipment she sees mountains in the distance, a lake nearby, and a stand of tall trees. Knowing that people enjoy mountains, lakes, and stately trees she gets out her zoom lens, photographs these three things, and drives away satisfied.

What's wrong with this picture? The photographer only noticed what she knew prospective visitors would like. Her zoom lens restricted her field of vision like a set of blinders so that she could see only what she already knew. No doubt there were some other features in the landscape that were both attractive to visitors and unique to that particular park, but she missed them by choosing to "look" at the park only through a single lens, and a narrow one at that.

A second photographer notices the same mountains, lake, and trees, and uses her zoom lens to record them as possible focal points for a pictorial spread. But she also wants to discover what else this place would offer. She now takes some shots with a wider-angle lens, framing first one panorama, then another. Then she just looks around as she strolls through the park. She learns that there are wildflowers that only exist in this park, rare animals, and rock formations unknown in most other places. Remembering her wide-angle shots, she thinks about which of those backgrounds would best fit these unique features. When she takes the camera out again she'll capture the flowers, animals, and rocks in a natural setting that offers the best background for them. Her pictures will portray things that make this park a good bet for mountain-and-lake-and-tree lovers, as well as those looking for something unusual. The pictures reflect, both for her and her magazine's readers, a much more thorough understanding of the place.

Landscape photography involves trying out different lenses, moving from distant shots to closeups to wide angles and back again, looking at the landscape from different perspectives in a search for the subtle as well as the obvious, for the unexpected features as well as the familiar. The photographer studies not only the landscape but also how useful each lens is in revealing that landscape. The process of classroom research is one of studying not just the classroom but also the questions that focus the study and the methods used to gather and analyze data. Research questions reflect assumptions about what's important; in other words, our theory about classrooms, students, language, learning, and teaching. Theory is a kind of lens. Through it we can only see what we presently know. But doing research means examining assumptions and putting theory at risk (Harste, Woodward, and Burke, 1984). Lucy Calkins (1985) describes doing research as asking ourselves what we're ultimately willing to believe. To ask that is to put our present theory at risk and look beyond our present beliefs to try to see more than our lens will currently let us see. Like photographers, researchers need to be willing to change their lenses, to entertain a different set of assumptions about what's important in order to see the classroom landscape differently.

Judith Green and Catherine Emihovich (1987) say that research methods are also lenses, in that each offers a different way of looking at a classroom and the goings on within it. Selecting a different method may give us a chance to look beyond our present beliefs; but we can only see what each lens will reveal. In a sense the real quest of a researcher is a search for those questions and methods that lead to new insights and deeper understanding. The story of such a quest is one of re-examination, of re-searching, looking again and again at our present understandings, our data, and the methods by which that data was gathered and reflected upon. When a researcher looks not just for what can be easily explained but for what defies explanation initial questions might be modified or abandoned and methods may be discarded in favor of others, adapted or even invented so that more can be learned.

QUESTIONS: WHERE DO THEY COME FROM?

Initial assumptions about what's important come partly from classroom experience. That experience generates questions that can launch a quest: Why do Jenny, Mark, and Russell seem to hate to read? Why is *A Day No Pigs Would Die* such a hit with urban students who have nothing in common with Rob Peck? Can third-graders really produce a class newspaper and will they learn useful things from doing it? Can I convince my undergraduates of the importance of reading good literature aloud in their classrooms? Why should kids who had no trouble learning to talk have such a terrible time learning to write? How can I include all the required content for my grade level, survive the teacher-evaluation process, and still keep language whole and meaningful for my class?

Questions also grow out of thoughtful reading of professional literature: Is it important for the teacher, as well as students, to bring a piece of writing to writing conferences, as Lucy Calkins (1986) suggests? Could a content reading lesson developed for secondary-school students by Joe Vaughan and Tom Estes (1985) be useful with fourth-graders and their social studies book? Will pen-pal letters from first-graders help my undergraduates better understand writing development, as described by Don Graves (1983) and others? How might students respond if I require them to keep a journal of their reactions to assigned reading?

Questions like these live in all our minds. Occasionally, they rise to the surface of our awareness. When they do, they signify the need to push beyond our present knowledge and find out whether what we now believe is really worth believing. Investigating these questions together can help us build individual and collective understanding of literacy and learning that we call theory, as well as provide better instruction.

But simply asking the question is the first step. How do we find the answers?

QUESTS: WHERE ARE THE ANSWERS?

Let's take one of these questions as an example. How might students respond if they were required to keep a journal of their reactions to assigned reading? Now we can describe how a teacher might do a naturalistic classroom study to find some answers, gain some insights into literacy and learning, and develop better instructional practice.

HOW DO WE FIND A FOCUS?

Just asking the question is an important first step, but the question alone doesn't give a researcher much direction. Since the question doesn't automatically give us any clear idea of what to look at or what to look for, researchers at this stage might feel more than a little uneasy about not having a clearer sense of how to proceed. But there are ways of dealing with this uneasiness.

One way is to develop some specific research questions to serve as an initial, tentative lens for observation and data-gathering. Researchers can refine a broad question to give themselves a data-gathering framework, being very careful to remember that while this framework can be a useful way of getting started, it can also be a powerful constraint on what will be learned.

Refining Questions: Deciding What to Look *At*

To illustrate how a question might be refined, think of the question: How might students respond to journal writing? A researcher can ask: "What do I mean by *respond*? What are some ways that kids could respond to doing reading journals that I'd consider important?" Suppose the researcher, drawing upon past teaching experience and knowledge of journal literature and conference presentations on this topic, decides that:

1. Students' written products, the journal entries themselves, could change in the course of a semester or a year.
2. Their use of the writing process could also change as journal writing proceeds.
3. Any changes seen in journal writing might show up in other writing as well.

Making these decisions suggests what the researcher might initially look at; namely, the journals themselves, the process of journal writing, and both the process and products involved in other writing.

Refining Questions: Deciding What to Look *For*

Deciding what to look for involves a little more thought about previous decisions. If both written products and students' use of the writing process might change, how might they be different? If changes could show up in other writing where might these appear? A classroom researcher, again drawing on personal experiences and the professional literature, might suspect that journal entries would become longer, more complex, and more varied in focus during the term; that students may begin to revise (or to revise more), engage in more prewriting activities, and share their writing more often for more purposes; and that these or other changes might show up in writing assignments done in class, in those done outside of class, or in any other student writing that may be available. Whether these suspicions are borne out or not, the researcher now has a sense of what to look for, at least in the beginning stages of the inquiry. The chart, "Framing and Refining Research Questions," on the next page illustrates the process of framing and refining research questions.

Data Sources: Deciding Where to Look

This question asking and decision making will help to direct our attention toward some potentially useful sources of data. The chart provides some possible data sources for Step 3 questions about reading journals.

Recording Data: Writing Field Notes

While this list of data sources may seem large, much of it (such as journals and other written work) already waits to be analyzed in a teacher's classroom. The rest of it (such as in-process writing behaviors, classroom interactions, and the observations of other teachers) is readily available to

Framing and Refining Research Questions

Step 1	Step 2	Step 3
	• Do their written products change?	• Do they become longer?
		• Do they become more complex?
		• Do the topics and themes change?
How do kids respond to journal writing?	• Does their use of the writing process change?	• Do they revise more than before?
		• Do they engage in any more prewriting?
		• Do they share their writing more?
		• For what purposes?
	• Do changes in journal writing show up in other writing?	• Do changes show up in in-class writing assignments?
		• Do changes show up in outside assignments?
		• Do changes show up in any other writing?

be recorded in the form of field notes taken by the researcher as time allows.

Writing field notes, like writing good class notes, is simply a matter of recording the important aspects of what was observed without trying to capture every single detail. Though a researcher may be anxious about losing information that could turn out to be important, most find that reading their field notes "brings back" in considerable detail the events they observed, so that potentially important information is preserved.

Field notes, then, have a dual purpose: to give observation data a tangible form so that it can be analyzed, and to help the researcher recall the entire scene that was observed and not just the specifics that were written down.

Classroom researchers usually write field notes as they observe. If they are simultaneously observing and working with their students they try to

Data Sources

Questions	Look At	Look For
Entries longer?	Student journals	Number of words per entry
Entries more complex?	Student journals	Indices of grammatical, semantic complexity
Entries more varied?	Student journals	Number and variety of topics or themes
More revision?	Journal writing	Instances of revision in process
	Student journals	Number, types, effectiveness of revisions
	Classroom talk	Informal interviews, conferences, class discussions, conversations
More prewriting?	Journal writing	Instances of prewriting in process
	Classroom talk	Informal interviews, conferences, class discussions, conversations
Writing shared?	Classroom talk	Informal interviews, conferences, class discussions, conversations
	Journal writing	Instances of sharing in process
Changes elsewhere?	Writing process (nonjournals)	Indicators of length, complexity, revision, prewriting, etc.
	Written products (nonjournals)	Indicators of length, complexity, etc.
	Writing process	Interviews with students, outside of class, other teachers

write notes as soon as possible after the observation period ends. When it isn't possible to record field notes during or immediately after an observation, or when intensive, repeated observation would be useful, audio and video recordings can be made.

Avoiding "Tunnel Vision": Casting Out a Big Net

Although it is certainly useful to have something definite to look at and to look for, we also need to remember June McConaghy's (1986) advice that researchers should not focus too narrowly, especially at the beginning of their investigations. What we can find out is limited by the questions we ask; and our questions are limited by what we know enough to ask. When research is too narrowly focused, we may end up like that first photographer—able to discover only what we already know.

In her first study June McConaghy followed a suggestion from an experienced researcher and "cast out a big net" to "record as much as possible the ordinary things I was seeing everyday" (p. 725). Taking time to observe and document events and activities that seem unrelated to our research questions is an important way of preventing the narrowness of "tunnel vision" that all researchers are susceptible to, a way of remaining open to new knowledge that lies beyond our experience and the professional literature we've read.

Casting out a big net in order to look beyond specified data sources is an important feature of any naturalistic study. Naturalistic researchers emphasize the idea that events are shaped by their contexts and only understandable in terms of those contexts. In order to understand students' responses to journal writing, then, we have to consider the other goings on in the classroom and the school, as well as what happens during journal writing.

Naturalistic researchers also emphasize the uniqueness of any classroom, and try to capture and understand it as well as its commonality with other situations. When we focus too narrowly it's easy to miss those unique features—and ultimately miss the chance to understand the situation in more than a superficial way.

DATA ANALYSIS: FINDING PATTERNS, NEW QUESTIONS, AND NEW PATTERNS

The process of analyzing data is one of looking for patterns and categories and refining them as more data becomes available. Whatever forms the data take and however it is recorded, the researcher needs to begin analyzing it immediately and continue to do so regularly.

Analyzing Data: Examining Our Questions

Both the initial questions that guide data-gathering and the initial patterns we see in the data are tentative. We need to examine both to help avoid tunnel vision. When researchers analyze data regularly, and continue to "cast out a big net" to keep looking beyond the data that directly addresses their specific questions, new questions often arise. These may turn out to be just as important as (or even more important than) the original ones. In fact, researchers who don't generate new questions or modify any in the course of their study should probably suspect that they've let their questions confine them too much, and that they haven't looked at their data thoroughly enough.

To explore this idea of new questions, imagine that the researcher who plans the journal-writing study is very interested in the writing process, and has taken courses, attended workshops and conference presentations, and read books and articles about it. Since the specific questions in our example all deal with writing, the study of reading response journals is really examining (at least in the beginning) only what the researcher already knows a lot about. There's no explicit attention being paid at the moment to what students are reading, or their responses to reading, or the impact of writing on these responses. If these matters are really important for a full understanding of what reading-response journals mean to students, and if they never occur to the researcher in the form of new questions to investigate, important insights will be missed and the researcher will know little more at the end of the study than at the beginning. This researcher, then, ends up like our first photographer—able to see nothing beyond what was already known.

But if a researcher regularly examines the data generated by research questions, and also asks, "What else do I see going on that might be important?", the study can be refined by new research questions that are developed and investigated as the study proceeds, and much more can be learned. Like the second photographer, this researcher can see and understand more at the end of the study by virtue of having consciously looked for more.

This same strategy can help us recognize unanticipated data sources that may be as valuable as the original ones. Parent conferences, for instance, could reveal some important things that are happening in students' writing and reading at home which the researcher ought to attend to.

Regular examination of the data also helps us recognize when our original research questions aren't as useful as we had thought they'd be, and see the need to modify or abandon them. For example, it may become apparent to a researcher studying journal writing that the question about length of entries is really insignificant. As we analyze the journals the first several times we may see that longer entries are consistently neither better nor worse than shorter ones; and length is consistently unrelated to students' fluency, their confidence and willingness to take risks, their attitudes about writing, or anything else of importance. At that point we should probably abandon the question of length, at least tentatively, and focus on more important things.

Analyzing Data: Managing the Volume

Another reason to analyze early and often is that otherwise the amount of data can become overwhelming. One thing is certain about data from a naturalistic classroom study: There'll be a great deal of it. If it's allowed to accumulate for too long without analysis the notes become meaningless and the sheer quantity of data makes a search for patterns and categories difficult if not impossible.

We suggest weekly analysis of data as a rule of thumb for the beginning of a study like this; and we'd quickly add that this schedule can and should be adjusted as needed. During an analysis session the researcher gathers the recorded data—in this case journals and other writings, field notes, and recordings, if any—and examines it to establish, expand, or amend categories and patterns of student response. Writing summaries of field notes and recordings can be helpful in this regard, and constructing charts to summarize data from journals and other pieces of writing can also be useful. Analysis sessions like this shouldn't take much more than an hour. Researchers might consider the time they spend as a guide to whether they're analyzing often enough.

PEER DEBRIEFING: WHO CAN HELP?

As soon as patterns start to emerge and categories begin to take shape researchers need to begin sharing them with colleagues as a way of checking their perceptions against those of other knowledgeable professionals. Teachers have always consulted each other, and these peer debriefing sessions are really no different. They are simply occasions for researchers to say to colleagues, "Here are my observations so far, and what I think they tell me. What do they look like to you?" As data and tentative findings are shared, colleagues will often confirm what the researcher has seen or inferred as valid and plausible, but sometimes they will see things the researcher may otherwise miss, or suggest alternative categories and patterns that deserve consideration.

Peer Debriefing: How It Helps

In a study of student responses to keeping reading journals a researcher might find a pattern of entries that relate story events or characters to the personal experiences of readers. A colleague, though, might look at the same journal entries and notice that these personal experiences all have to do with problems of growing up, regardless of the events or characters referred to in the stories that were read. Later in the same study the researcher might examine records of observed journal-writing episodes and tentatively categorize these observations in terms of how much revision students are doing in their individual entries. The researcher may group entries according to whether they indicate extensive revision, some revision, or no revision by students. A colleague in a debriefing session, however, might suggest that although some students make no overt revisions during writing, their subsequent entries are in fact revisions of earlier ones.

In each of these situations the researcher must decide whether or not to act on this input from colleagues, and what specific action to take.

Sometimes researchers decide to revise tentative categories or perceived patterns exactly as colleagues suggest; sometimes they decide to trust their own first judgments; and at other times they are led to new insights that go beyond both their observations and that of their colleagues. Whatever the decision, final conclusions can be drawn with more confidence because they are tested against and informed by the judgment of others.

Peer Debriefing: When and How

Peer debriefing should occur periodically throughout the course of a study, but the frequency of sessions is really an individual matter. We think it's important to debrief regularly; and we've found weekly sessions useful in a number of situations. But because a weekly session is neither feasible nor desirable in all situations, we suggest that researchers establish a tentative debriefing schedule and then adjust it as needed.

In a sense peer debriefing sessions consist of researchers being questioned about the patterns in their data, tentative findings, and interpretations. Though a colleague may simply propose a different interpretation or describe a different pattern they see in the data rather than ask questions, the effect is the same—the researcher must re-search, looking again at data and interpretations from a new or altered perspective. Since the questions a colleague does ask can be very important and useful, we've listed some general questions that have proved helpful in our experience. The questions are in no particular order; and they aren't meant to be comprehensive. They're intended as examples of questions that can be powerful in the examination and re-examination of data.

1. What doesn't fit?
2. What doesn't make sense?
3. Are you sure?
4. How else could you explain it?
5. Did you look for other patterns?
6. Does this always happen?
7. What does this remind you of?
8. Why? Why not?

FIELD NOTES, SUMMARIES, AND THE RESEARCHER'S LOG: WHY WRITE?

Like many others we're convinced of the value of writing as a vehicle for discovery and a way of learning. Writing is always a process of selection, of deciding what we choose to say and how we choose to say it. Both kinds of decisions require reflection: What did I just see? What does my data show? What might I have overlooked? How can I best state the questions that have been nagging at me, so I can try to address them?

Though we may ponder these matters without pencil and paper there's no question that writing about them forces us into decisions. As we jot down field notes, or write summaries of our notes, or work on a draft of our research report, we make decisions about what we've seen and what it means. We discover what we know and believe as we write, thinking ahead to what we'll say next and simultaneously looking back at what's already been said. We also learn as we make new connections. Captured on paper, both our discovered knowledge and our fresh insights can be revisited and revised as needed.

Chapter 2 documents the change and growth of Leslie's thoughts, conclusions, and insights into the questions she asked. As the research was conducted and the data were analyzed, it was the process of writing that really helped formulate and crystallize her thoughts. As she talked to John, Sharon, and other teachers about the data she was gathering and the results she was finding, new ideas and conclusions came to her. Though she valued and gained insight from peer debriefing, it was through writing, transacting with her ideas in print, that she pushed her own thinking into new avenues, faced a dilemma, and came to terms with it.

Writing can certainly help solve problems that arise in the course of a research project. Classroom studies with multiple data sources, for example, often involve conflicting findings when the data from two or more sources give very different pictures of what's happening. These conflicts have to be resolved. We have to figure out which sources we should trust the most and why. In her study, Leslie was confronted with such a conflict between data from observations of regular classroom writing activities and data from pre- and postwriting samples and a writing attitude measure. By writing about these conflicts she was able not only to resolve them but also to make new discoveries about research and the relative usefulness of different kinds of data (Patterson, 1987), discoveries that have since been incorporated by other classroom researchers.

Periodically examining what's been written—field notes, summaries, drafts—to ask: "What else is going on?", to look for alternate interpretations, and to consider other data sources is an invaluable way to keep theory at risk and look at data and methods from alternate perspectives. This process of revisiting and reconsidering previous decisions is also one of decision making. It, too, can be enhanced by writing. Keeping a log as a record of that process allows for discovery and learning; as we make entries in a research log we "peer-debrief" with ourselves, taking on stances and viewpoints that are different from those we held earlier so we can see and examine other perspectives. Writing an entry we again discover what we know at that point and forge new connections, all of which will be available for consideration later as we determine the conclusions of our work.

PROFESSIONAL LITERATURE: WHAT DOES IT OFFER?

As suggested earlier, professional literature—books, journal articles, workshops, and conference presentations—are important sources of research questions. Now we want to emphasize the meaningfulness of using this professional literature in the process of analyzing data and drawing conclusions.

Whatever research questions are asked, they can be examined in the light of published theories of literacy and learning and in terms of previous research that explores questions similar to our own. Like a good colleague this literature can give us new perspectives and interpretive frameworks that sometimes reinforce and sometimes challenge our thinking. In consulting this literature, and accepting the challenges it may provide, we make both our studies and ourselves more powerful.

We don't mean to suggest that published research and theory is necessarily conclusive, or that a researcher's conclusions are wrong if they differ with published work, or that a classroom study is not valid unless the researcher is able to cite dozens of previous studies. To suggest that is to assume that absolute knowledge is to be found in journals and books, an anti-intellectual stance that stops the quest for new knowledge in its tracks. What we do suggest is that ignoring what others have seen and thought is also fundamentally anti-intellectual. To consider the ideas and data shared in the literature critically is to be willing to look beyond ourselves and our present knowledge and put our theory at risk.

CLASSROOM RESEARCH: WHY IS IT POWERFUL?

Classroom studies can be powerful. The data come from authentic classroom settings. The multiple data sources in a classroom and "next-door" colleagues, as well as those known only through their professional writing, offer different perspectives, different lenses for exploring our landscapes. Conclusions result from a search for unity and pattern in the data, a search that includes the researcher's colleagues and the opportunities they provide for seeing things in a new way.

Researchers looking for answers in their classrooms can become the leaders of our profession. They can lead by reformulating theory in terms of real kids in real classrooms with real teachers. They can lead by showing that theory lives, not just in scholarly texts but in our own minds and motives. They can lead by demonstrating that the best way to improve instruction is to put theory at risk by constantly observing the living data in every classroom. Finally, they can lead by realizing that researchers are themselves part of that living data, and by sharing the greater self-awareness that comes from classroom research.

The profession needs the leadership of teacher researchers. As teachers we already have important questions—questions that are the beginnings of new knowledge and a renewed profession. As researchers we can find equally important answers.

3. Teaching, Researching, and Problem Solving

Leslie Patterson

I stand at the doorway of my classroom before third period, thinking about our writing workshop activities this week, as students prepare pieces for the first classroom anthology. I will juggle students' questions and try to keep everyone on task. In addition to their anthology pieces, the students will be working on weekly dialogue journals and on pen-pal letters, as well as reading a library book during spare minutes. The noise in the hall fades to the background as I turn to answer Misty's question. Misty has taken her books to her desk and brings me a rough draft of her next letter to Scott, her pen pal. She wants me to help her proofread it.

Misty has come a long way in the few short weeks since the beginning of school. Her first writing assignment, a letter to a freshman, was agony for her. She couldn't think of anything to say. The second day we worked on it she was in tears because she still hadn't really begun. After I sat with her, guiding her through a mapping activity to prewrite, she finally wrote a rough draft and then a final copy. Her final copy was neatly written, with only a few omitted words and usage problems. It had six sentences, all starting the same way. Although it sounded stiff and artificial to me, Misty had been extremely proud of it and was eager to receive a reply.

Misty's writing continued to improve, especially her letters and dialogue journals. First, her letters became longer, and she began using a variety of sentence patterns, which made her style much more spontaneous and interesting. She began rereading her drafts, making significant revisions. In her letters she began asking questions—questions for which she expected answers. Misty was using written language to communicate (Patterson, 1987).

As a writer Misty began that year afraid, disenfranchised, angry, isolated. Pen-pal letters gave Misty a vehicle through which she could begin to take risks, communicate with others, and explore her own potential as a language user. Those pen-pal letters helped Misty focus on personal goals for communicating. They provided a concrete context, one that held powerful personal meanings for her. This was a context that allowed her to experiment with linguistic and stylistic choices, much like the supportive context within which young children develop their oral language. For Misty, the pen-pal letters provided a context for building her own self-esteem and through which she could become more conscious of her own authoring decisions. Through letter writing Misty learned how to learn to be a better writer.

That is what pen-pal letters did for Misty, and classroom research did something similar for me. Before I began seeing myself as a researcher much of my instructional decision making was without conscious thought —a matter of gut reaction, probably some mixture of intuition, common sense, and my notion of what other teachers might do in the same situation. I didn't feel particularly confident or proud of the decisions I was making; I was frustrated and perhaps a little angry and isolated, because I felt that much of what I did was driven by the decisions "they" made in the principal's office, in the central administration building, and in the state legislature. I feel differently now. I came to know my students better, to know more about how they learn and how to support them in their efforts.

The systematic decision making required by classroom inquiry forced me to examine my instructional decisions, to evaluate them in the light of my emerging theoretical base and my growing knowledge of other researchers' decisions. Like Misty, I began to take control of my decisions, to invest more of myself in the whole enterprise, and to grow enormously in the process. Through research I learned how to learn to be a better teacher.

The study I conducted in my high-school English class during the 1984–1985 school year illustrates that process. The questions I had to answer as I planned and conducted that study are probably similar to those that other novice teacher researchers must face. My questions and answers are not necessarily the correct ones but this description of my search for answers may help others do their own exploring.

Initially, my purpose in the study was to describe students' responses to writing instruction that was much different from the product-centered instruction I had been depending on for six years of English teaching. I had become intrigued with the potentials I saw in the use of real communication for writing instruction. I wanted to provide real audiences for students and then to serve as a resource for them as they explored ways to communicate within those authentic situations. Specifically, Shirley Brice Heath and Amanda Branscombe's (1987) use of letter writing and Donald Graves' focus on process (1983) served as springboards for my research questions. My original research questions focused on student responses:

1. Do the students' writing products change? If so, how?
2. How do the students participate in the writing process? Does the nature of that participation change during the year? If so, how?
3. Do students' feelings about writing change? If so, how?
4. Do students of varying achievement levels respond to the proposed instruction differently? If so, how?

I had five sections of students—the three twelfth-grade classes were designated as low-achievers on the basis of standardized test scores or previous achievement in English classes; two other classes were combined tenth-, eleventh-, and twelfth-graders who had been identified as gifted language learners according to the district's assessment matrix. I was eager to see how these two groups of students, with dramatically different academic histories, responded to real audiences for their writing.

During the course of the study I learned about how these students responded to real audiences, but, like Misty's learning to write as she wrote pen-pal letters, I also learned about the process and the tools of research as I collected and analyzed the data. Complexities and ambiguities became apparent, and in the process of resolving those issues I learned a great deal about research. My graduate courses and my experienced colleagues provided invaluable input as I planned this study, but my own problem solving during the study itself was a powerful learning experience that gave substance to the concepts and the advice I had heard before.

The questions I had to address seemed to fall into five categories:

1. finding a focus
2. developing a design
3. selecting the data sources
4. establishing rigor
5. writing the report.

I am not offering these categories as a comprehensive guide to conducting classroom research or as an original contribution to the literature but as a summary of what I learned from this one study and as an illustration that the classroom can provide an exciting learning context for teacher researchers.

FINDING A FOCUS

Finding a focus is perhaps the most difficult task a teacher researcher must face. The classroom offers too many intriguing possibilities to be addressed in any one study, and it was difficult for me to narrow my focus to a single aspect of the process. The research questions listed above didn't narrow my focus very much—those questions attempted to address changes in the actual writing products and the students' use of the process, as well as their attitudes and feelings about writing and about themselves as writers. The research questions suggest that those changes would be documented for all the students across a full school year, and also that students' changes in the two achievement levels would be compared and contrasted.

I was just beginning to understand what a process approach to writing instruction might mean within a secondary-school classroom; and it was difficult for me to look at one aspect of the process by itself. In fact, it was the holistic nature of the approach that was most intriguing to me. I couldn't conceive of how a researcher could focus on just one part of the process of language learning. I didn't know any ways to focus on a single aspect without violating what I saw as the integrity of the whole, and that meant I had to collect a mountain of data. In reality, it meant that the data analysis and writing actually took two additional years after the first nine months of instruction and data collection. That is a significant investment of time and energy, and if I had not chosen this study as a dissertation topic I might not have finished it. Because of the time involved in data analysis and writing, a more defined focus is perhaps advisable for many teacher researchers.

Sometimes the purpose of the particular study can serve to focus it. For example, teacher researchers may conduct studies in order to solve particular problems, an approach that is sometimes called "action research." In that case the nature of the problem under study would determine the focus of the research questions and would have an effect on the selection of data sources. Teacher researchers may also conduct studies to replicate or extend published studies. In such a case the focus and design of the original study will determine many research decisions.

A consideration of the ultimate purpose of the study and its intended audience may suggest a focus. The context of the entire research situation will affect the researcher's decisions. For example, if the findings will eventually be used as school-district policies are considered or implemented, that may affect the design of the study. If the teacher researcher is planning to present the findings at a professional conference, the research decisions might be different.

During the process of data analysis I began to see some ways that a researcher could focus on particular aspects of a holistic process within a data-rich classroom. These are the issues I now consider as I plan classroom studies; these are the issues that help me define an initial focus, always with the understanding that a different focus may finally emerge as being more significant or more helpful.

Group Trends or Individual Growth?

Usually, a teacher researcher's focus is on the growth of individual students, because teachers know their students as individuals rather than as a group of third-graders or seventh-graders. Teacher researchers, however, sometimes decide to use group measures—class averages of test scores or attitude inventories—to compare the ways groups of students respond to different methods. As a novice teacher researcher I assumed that I should use group data because many of the published research findings I knew of were reported in terms of group means. I soon decided that I was more interested in individual growth—the puzzles and the anomalies—rather than group trends.

At the beginning of a study it may be helpful for teacher researchers to decide whether group or individual information would be more helpful by considering the ultimate purpose of their particular studies.

Still Photography or Moving Pictures?

Another issue to consider is whether the study is to provide a static picture of students at a particular point in time or whether it is more desirable to explore the changes that occur over time. The purpose of classic ethnography is to describe a culture or a group at one point in time in order to answer the question: What is it like to be a member of this group? The ethnography tends to resemble still photography or portraiture (Lightfoot, 1983). Although my study employed ethnographic methodologies, such as interviews and participant observation, I was concerned about documenting changes over time. Because I wanted to describe those changes I included both September and May writing samples and writing apprehension questionnaires, quantitative data, and field notes that recorded students' ongoing responses. As I analyzed the data I realized that the pre- and postinstructional measures of writing and attitudes did not always yield the same findings and conclusions as the field notes. I realized that each of these approaches offers particular advantages and challenges, and that teacher researchers who consider all the options will make decisions appropriate to their own studies.

Products or Process?

Closely related to the issue of still photography versus moving pictures is the decision about whether to focus on the processes or the products of learning. The teacher researcher may be interested in describing and analyzing students' products—tests, writing products, attitude measures, and so on—or in describing students' participation in the learning processes—planning, conferencing, self-correction, etc. Either focus is viable, and either could yield significant findings. They are obviously interconnected and may be documented and analyzed in the same study, but it is important for the teacher researcher to think about the differences between product and process in relation to the purpose of the study, to articulate research questions that help define the study and point to appropriate data sources.

Teaching or Learning?

Although the distinction between teaching and learning may be a subtle one teacher researchers should probably consider whether they are more interested in exploring how teachers teach or how learners learn. Either would be a valid focus for study and could offer significant findings, but choosing one focus might make further research decisions clearer.

DEVELOPING A DESIGN

Teacher researchers often ask questions dealing with research design:

Do I need a control group?
Should I include pre- and posttests, or pre- and postwriting samples?
Should I depend on quantitative data and statistical analyses?

Those questions come from a familiarity with experimental or quasi-experimental research where findings report the results of some comparison—an experimental group to a control or preintervention scores to posttest scores. Because much of the research we read follows these kinds of designs novice teacher researchers may assume they are necessary.

Within the experimental paradigm in which educational research has generally been conducted, the generalizability of these findings and conclusions rest on the soundness of the design. For example, if treatments are assigned randomly or if subjects are randomly selected and assigned to treatment groups, the findings are thought to be generalizable. If pre- and postinstruments and procedures have been validated in other studies the findings are also more persuasive.

Teacher researchers must consider those issues in relation to their dual roles as teachers and researchers. As I face these kinds of methodological decisions I am first a teacher, then a researcher; so my research decisions can never interfere with my students' opportunities to learn and my research decisions can never contradict my instructional theory base.

For that reason I choose not to compare an experimental treatment to a control; I choose not to depend primarily on pre- and posttests for data about student growth; and I choose to collect data over a long period of time. In short, I choose a naturalistic design rather than an experimental one. First, I am interested in documenting the complexities of *how* a theory-based instructional approach works with individual students, rather than in simply establishing that it *does* work. Second, the decision not to use control groups becomes an ethical question: I wouldn't waste students' time by trying a treatment that I thought might not "work," and I wouldn't withhold a theory-based instructional approach from a control group in order to establish that it is, in fact, effective.

Fortunately an alternative research paradigm, often called naturalistic research, is gaining credibility among educational researchers, particularly in literacy research. The assumptions underlying the naturalistic research paradigm are generally consistent with the assumptions underlying holistic, process-oriented approaches to reading and writing instruction. For example, naturalistic researchers try to study authentic learning within real contexts. They try to include data over a long period of time rather than in short interventions. They view the researcher as a primary research instrument, so that the teacher researcher's observations become critical in the collection and analysis of data. The naturalistic research paradigm does not require control groups, nor does it require random assignment of experimental treatments. The naturalistic research paradigm also offers teacher researchers methodological choices that do not disrupt the instructional process, the teacher's primary concern.

SELECTING THE DATA SOURCES

When educational researchers discuss data collection they often debate the comparative merits of qualitative and quantitative data. For the teacher researcher that is often a useless distinction. Teachers and researchers need both kinds of data. They need qualitative data—descriptions and narratives about what happens in the classroom—and they need quantitative data—scores from tests, analysis of writing products, results from attitude questionnaires. To reduce data selection to a simplistic choice between qualitative and quantitative data is to establish a misleading and harmful dichotomy.

In my study of communication-based composition instruction I had identified a variety of data sources, both quantitative and qualitative, each of which addressed one or more of the research questions:

Changes in student writing products	Field notes
	Writing folders
	Pre- and postwriting samples
	Dialogue journals
Changes in their use of the writing process	Field notes

Changes in students' attitudes	Field notes
	Pre- and postquestionnaires
Differences between low- and high-achievers	All of the above

As I began to analyze the data I realized that some of the data sources seemed to contradict others. For example, Table 3.1 reports the analysis of the pre- and postwriting samples. It shows that in terms of the number of total words in high-achievers' writing samples, their fluency had increased by 200 percent—quite impressive. From my knowledge of their individual writing folders, however, I knew that their fluency had not really increased that much but that their fluency, in terms of the length of their writings, was closely related to the purpose of specific messages. To be effective some messages must be longer than others. The data from the pre- and postwriting samples contradicted the data from the writing folders. My dilemma was, how do I draw conclusions from findings that seem to be contradictory?

Another example was the writing apprehension questionnaires reported

Table 3.1.

Summary of the Writing Product Analysis, Low and High Achievers' Holistic Ratings, Fluency, Elaboration, and Conventionality

	High-achievers			Low-achievers		
	September	May	Difference	September	May	Difference
Holistic rating (5-point scale)	2.4	3.0	+ 0.6	1.9	2.0	+0.1
Fluency (total words)	123.0	244.5	+121.5	89.2	98.0	+ 8.8
Fluency (total t-units)*	12.4	10.1	− 2.3	12.4	13.6	+1.2
Elaboration (words per t-unit)	9.9	24.2	+ 14.3	7.2	7.2	0
Conventionality (nonconventionalities per 100 words)	1.5	1.2	− 0.3	11.0	7.8	− 3.2

*T-units—thought units (Hunt, 1965) are the smallest segments of written language that can stand alone syntactically. They are similar to *independent clauses*. An increase in the number of t-units in a writer's work over time is viewed as a sign of growth.

in Table 3.2. One of the prompts on the questionnaire was "I find it easy to write well." The students were to respond on a five-point scale from "strongly agree" to "strongly disagree." It would appear that as students' attitudes toward writing became more positive they would find it easier to write. Just the opposite seemed to be true for high-achievers. According to my observations and other prompts in that questionnaire, their writing apprehension generally decreased during the year, but on that one prompt they responded that they found it more difficult to write in May than they

Table 3.2.
Low Achievers' Changes in Writing Apprehension from May to September, Reported as Percentage of Responses that Moved Either in a *Positive* Direction (Indicating Less Writing Apprehension) or *Negative* Direction (Indicating More Writing Apprehension).

Prompt	Positive change (in percents)	Negative change (in percents)	Net change
I enjoy writing.	− 3	+ 1	negative
I find it easy to write well.	+12	+ 6	mixed
I don't like to write very much.	+14	+ 7	mixed
Writing is a lot of fun.	+12	−11	positive
I avoid writing in school when I can.	+21	− 5	positive
I like to have my teacher read what I have written.	+12	−12	positive
I don't like to have my teacher grade my writing.	+12	− 5	positive
I feel good when I turn in my writing to my teacher.	+13	+ 1	positive
I worry when my teacher says my class is going to take a writing test.	+ 7	− 8	positive
I like to have my friends read what I have written.	+12	−32	positive
I'm not very good at writing.	+11	−16	positive
I don't think I write as well as other students.	+ 7	−13	positive
I look forward to writing my ideas down.	+ 9	−16	positive
I don't like to do a whole lot of writing.	+ 2	− 4	positive

had in September. A possible explanation is that as the high-achievers developed a more sophisticated notion of the writing process they did, in fact, decide that it was difficult to write well. A simplistic and uncritical acceptance of that one data source, the writing apprehension questionnaire, would have been misleading.

These are two examples of situations in which my comparisons of data from various sources prompted more questions than answers. I now understand how common that is during the research process. In order to integrate all the data into a coherent whole I had to make some decisions about prioritizing the findings from various data sources. And in order to do that I had to think through the theoretical and philosophical assumptions of both my instructional approach and the research methodologies I had chosen.

That analysis suggested that some of my choices of research methodologies were, in fact, contradictory to what I believed about the writing process. For example, my theoretical assumptions were that reading, writing, and learning are dynamic, transactional processes within specific social contexts (Harste, Woodward, and Burke, 1984b). If that is true my attempts to measure writing apprehension and writing effectiveness at any single point in time were perhaps a little silly. How valid is a questionnaire, a self-report on fourteen questions during the first and last weeks of school? I realized that such a questionnaire may yield information that can be helpful in describing a large group, but it is of questionable value in describing precisely how Misty feels about herself as a writer across a variety of contexts. If I believe that reading, writing, and learning are transactional processes, then I should attempt to gather data within authentic contexts in which students are communicating with real audiences. That's why my field notes seemed to yield the most helpful, the most powerful findings; and that's why the data from the questionnaires and the writing samples—both contrived situations—were the least useful. On that basis I generated categories of data sources to help me integrate my findings into some coherent conclusions. These categories are what I called contexts for data-gathering.

I gathered primary data from actual, authentic *transactions* between and among the students and me. Secondary data came from the *products* of those transactions; and tertiary data came from *cued responses* like the questionnaires and writing samples. Whenever a contradiction arose,

	Context A Authentic transactions	Context B Products of transactions	Context C Cued responses about transactions
Data-gathering methods	Observations (may be open-ended or highly structured)	Writing products Artifacts Open-ended interviews	Tests Questionnaires Attitude measures Highly structured interviews Writing samples
Intervening components	Researcher's knowledge and bias Data-analysis categories Observation instrument (if used)	Researcher's knowledge and bias Data-analysis categories	Researcher's knowledge and bias Data-analysis categories Data-gathering instruments
Report of findings (may be either qualitative or quantitative; with or without statistical analysis)	May attempt to recreate the experience for the reader or analyze the transaction with emic or etic categories	Analysis of artifacts or products for evidence about the original transactions	Analysis of cued responses for evidence about transactions

the authentic, transactional data sources would carry more weight. That was my rationale for relying most heavily on field notes as I came to my final conclusions and as I wrote my final report.

As I sorted through my data and the related literature in order to come to that decision I learned a great deal about various approaches to research. The process of data analysis forced me to look at the information from a different perspective. It forced me to think through the theoretical and philosophical assumptions of research paradigms. It forced me to look for the essential characteristics and the potential contributions of both qualitative and quantitative data, of both natural and contrived research contexts. Analyzing the data in this one study taught me as much as any research course could have.

ESTABLISHING RIGOR

In choosing the naturalistic paradigm over the more familiar experimental paradigm I sacrificed what many researchers see as rigor—validity, reliability, and the generalizability of my findings. Those researchers may not be aware that the naturalistic paradigm has its own rigor—procedures to insure the credibility of its findings. Because I chose to document as closely as possible what was actually happening in my classroom the study had what researchers call ecological validity. It was a real classroom; I was the teacher; the data was collected as a part of the ongoing instruction during the entire year. The students' responses could be attributed to transactions within that instructional context, rather than to responses within a contrived experimental context.

I collected data for the entire school year so that the patterns I saw were validated over a long period of time, not just for a matter of days or weeks.

I looked to a variety of data sources for answers to each research question. The different data sources served to triangulate one another. For example, I watched for changes in students' feelings about writing in my field notes, in their dialogue journals, and in their responses to the writing apprehension questionnaire. If researchers see the same pattern emerging in three different kinds of data, they can trust that the pattern must be real and may be significant.

Finally, I checked my perceptions of the data through *member checks,* when I told students what I thought I was seeing and asked them to respond; and through peer debriefings, when I shared my findings and conclusions with colleagues to see whether they agreed with my interpretations. These discussions served as a checks-and-balances system for my naturalistic research and were invaluable to me.

Another issue that concerns experimental researchers is objectivity—based on the assumption that the researcher should make every effort to correct for personal biases in the collection and analysis of data. Personal relationships between the teacher and students preclude that kind of objectivity, but naturalistic researchers claim that scientific objectivity is an illusion, that all researchers have *a priori* beliefs and assumptions that affect their selection of data sources, their decisions about the design of studies, and their data-analysis processes. Rather than attempting to achieve objectivity, naturalistic researchers attempt to make their *a priori* beliefs and assumptions—their theoretical rationales—as explicit as possible, so the reader of the research can consider the final conclusions in light of the researcher's perspective.

WRITING THE REPORT

I had to decide how to report my findings. After all, I had descriptions of over 100 students for a full school year. I had my field notes, the students' writing folders, their grades, their attendance records, and their dialogue journals. What should I include in the report? How could I integrate the data into a coherent whole that would communicate to readers what the classroom experience had been like?

I could organize the report as answers to the stated research questions. Yes, the students' writing improved. Yes, their participation in the writing process changed. Yes, their feelings about writing improved. Yes, there were a few differences between the responses of the low-achievers and the high-achievers. But even more important, it seemed to me, was what I was learning about the culture of a writing workshop, the network of transactions among students as they became communities of learners. I wanted my research report to communicate that to my readers; and it seemed that straightforward answers to the stated research questions would not say anything about these complex and fascinating transactions.

About that time John Stansell suggested that I read Sara Lawrence Lightfoot's *The Good High School* (1983). To show her readers what it was like to be in those high schools, Lightfoot used what she called a portrait, a narrative of one day in each of the four schools she was studying. Everything she included in the portrait was actual data, but it was condensed into the span of one day. I decided that the portrait might help me show my students' responses to communication-based writing instruction.

From the first week of data collection I had written a weekly narrative for each class. I had used my field notes to trigger memories of critical incidents from each day—incidents that were interesting because they were typical of students' responses or because they were totally unexpected—anomalies. To create the portraits I took incidents from these weekly narratives within both low- and high-achieving classes, and wrote a narrative of one period in a low-achieving class and one in a high-achieving class. All of the incidents actually happened, but they didn't necessarily happen on the same day or during the same class period. The purpose of the portraits was to let readers experience what it was like to be in those classes on a typical day during the first few weeks of the school year.

Eventually I took the field notes and narratives from the second semester and compiled a low-achievers' portrait and a high-achievers' portrait for the end of the year. It seemed that the portraits told the reader much more about the students' responses than tables and figures could have. The description of Misty that introduces this chapter is an excerpt from one of those portraits.

CONCLUSION

The problem solving required by this classroom study forced me to learn more about my philosophical and theoretical assumptions, about the particular research context of my study, and about various methodological alternatives. The result was that I became a better researcher. Because I was doing research in my own classroom each research decision was also, directly or indirectly, an instructional decision. I was becoming a more confident and competent researcher at the same time that I was helping Misty and others become more confident and competent writers. Through classroom research I was learning how to learn to be a better teacher. And isn't that the ultimate goal of all educational research?

II

PRODUCT: THEORY

4. Building Theories

Teachers who ask questions and carry out inquiries in their classrooms seem to develop explanations of how students learn and how language works—their personal theories of teaching and learning. Many teacher researchers tell us that the process of researching led them to new theoretical insights. These insights invariably lead to theory building.

Theory building and research support and extend each other. In fact, the two processes work in concert to such an extent that we really shouldn't talk about how research *leads* to theory building but about how the two develop simultaneously. We see them as two facets of the same process, in much the same way that we have come to recognize reading and writing as two aspects of the language and thinking processes.

As we watch researching teachers we notice that the process of inquiry becomes almost as important as the content of the research itself. The results, data, and conclusions are important because they answer the questions that prompted the research project in the first place. But it is the process that is critical. In the midst of research decision making teachers deal with both theoretical and practical issues, and their questions turn to quests.

Perhaps a story of one teacher's quest would demonstrate the power of that process. Karen Saunders is a Chapter 1 reading teacher in a K-6 elementary school in Sioux Falls, South Dakota. She is responsible for about fifty students weekly and supervises three instructional aides who help with the teaching. As a result of a graduate course in middle-school reading Karen decided to try some methods, ask some questions, and watch her students. Her questions began as many other teacher researchers' questions begin; she made an observation: "I noticed that the better readers [in my class] are more verbal in their responses and are better able to communicate their ideas."

Although this observation does not seem particularly revolutionary it was something that interested Karen. She works with a variety of students in her role as a Chapter 1 teacher and sees many students who have been identified as having reading problems. Her observation is one that many teachers may have had before, but this one led her to a specific focus: "I wonder if there is a strong relationship between spoken language and reading ability." This wondering naturally led Karen to investigate what was going on in her classroom in terms of reading, responding, and learning: "I decided to do some research to compare the [verbal] responses of good readers and poor readers [during class discussion]."

As Karen observed her students working, took notes in her classroom, and generally became more aware of the data from the class, she began to watch her students and herself more. "I was suddenly aware of the speech around me," she wrote in a weekly journal. She began to think of herself as a researcher. In another note in her journal she commented: "I'll have to wait another week to report any trends."

Karen was on a quest. She knew she was searching for an answer to the question she had formulated, but it wasn't until most of the data was collected and analyzed that she realized she was also on the road to building stronger personal theory as a result of that search:

I don't want to sound wishy-washy, but I guess that I have been influenced by most of the major trends that have been around since [the early 1970's]. I read [Jeanne] Chall and added a strong phonics approach for young readers; I read about accountability and taught study skills and test-taking skills; I read about school effectiveness and adopted more direct teaching in my approach. So I suppose that it's only natural that I would give whole language a try, too. I've taken a few classes, read about a dozen books, tried out some techniques. But this time there have been two experiences that I feel will make a lasting impact.

The first of these was the experience of actually being in a [graduate] class that was run as a reading workshop. My observations, my notes, and my ideas helped to formulate a strong understanding of the theory.

The second experience was establishing an explicit theory of reading. In all my studies and experiences with reading, I never really felt a need to have a thought-out theory of reading which I could use to determine the effectiveness of the methods with which I was being bombarded . . . with an explicit theory of language before me, I feel great freedom to select techniques from whole language, direct teaching methods, or phonics games.

Karen is building a theory—a rationale for instructional decision making—as a result of being engaged in the process of doing research in her classroom. It was no accident that the research and the theory building happened at the same time. The two processes belong together. They support each other; and they support Karen, who now recognizes that she is a much better teacher as a result of all the work that she did and all of the insights she gained.

Karen is just one example of a teacher who is building theoretical understandings as a result of research. We have watched others; and we have read the work of teacher researchers in the pages of professional books and journals. From watching teachers like Karen and talking to them about the insights they achieved while making decisions and conducting research, we can make some observations about the process of building personal theory.

HOW DO WE BUILD THEORIES?

As a result of an extensive study in which she interviewed a variety of language teachers, Sharon learned something about how teachers build theories. The models she developed have been helpful for us in discussions of theory building. We hope they prove helpful to you as you discuss them in your circle of learners.

Traditionally, the way the educational community has defined theory was based on the Newtonian-era view of theory building and hypothesis testing. This traditional view of theory building looked something like this:

Ideal theory
(Truth)
↑
Theory
↑
Research
↑
Researcher

Figure 4.1
Traditional view of theory building.

This view of theory building begins with two assumptions: that knowledge is absolute, and that it exists apart from the knower. Given those assumptions, educational researchers work to discover the unchanging laws that govern human learning by observing the behavior of learners and teachers. They observe under rigorously controlled conditions, so that behavior will clearly reflect those unchanging laws.

Researchers can start building an educational theory by being careful to keep their hunches and biases rigidly controlled so that what is "really out there" can be verified and examined without being corrupted by what someone "merely thinks." Educational theory comes from using logic to infer some underlying principles that explain behavior. This theory is then examined against more behavior; *a priori* hypotheses are tested in formal ways that seek to prevent the researcher from introducing any biases that will distort the "true reality" under investigation. The traditional goal of theory building, then, is to approximate more and more closely the laws of nature.

In order to build theory, though, researchers must first have explicit knowledge of existing theory—the best approximation so far. They must also be rigorously trained in approved methods of scientific research, methods that depersonalize the inquiry process by insulating the researcher in order to gather and analyze data as objectively as possible. No wonder that for decades the study of children in school closely resembled the study of rows of sweet potatoes.

When an educational theory from this tradition is developed enough to present in a text, classroom teachers are expected to adopt and apply it without modification as an accurate account of the way things really are. Modifications or adaptations that teachers might make would be departures from "true theory" in the text, and from the "true knowledge" it tries to represent.

This traditional view of theory building tends to ignore the teacher's role in instructional decision making. We see the teacher's personal theory or rationale as critical. That *personal* theory is the result of transactions with students, with fellow teachers, and with published advice about teaching and learning. This leads us to an alternative view of theory building—a transactional approach to instructional theory building (Lee and Patterson, 1988). This view of theory building is based on the work of Dewey and Bentley (1949), in which they describe "knowing" as a transaction in which the "knower" and the "known" are not separate but inseparable. Rosenblatt's work (1978, 1985) also reflects this understanding of *transaction*. In her description of literary experience she points out that the meaning of a book is actually a result of the transaction between a particular reader and a particular text. This is different from the traditional view of literary explication in which the meaning is believed to reside in the text. Likewise, a transactional view of theory building differs from the traditional view where knowledge is separate from learners and theory exists in texts for direct adoption by the teacher.

A transactional view of theory building would recognize theory as an evolving, personal rationale for instructional decision making. It would look something like this:

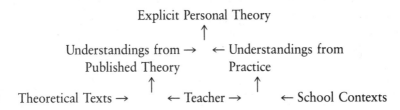

Figure 4.2
Transactional view of theory building.

Figure 4.2 shows that explicit personal theory is a result of a teacher's transactions both with theoretical texts and with school contexts that include students, colleagues, and parents. In this view theory is a unique experience, an event. It does not exist "out there" in a text but is created and developed from our many transactions with what's "out there"—theoretical texts, students, other teachers. When teachers read a theoretical text the result of that transaction is personal theory, shaped by their unique experiences and alive only in their hearts and minds. Because we hold this view we encourage teachers to read theoretical works, watch their students and other teachers, and listen to experts—just as advocates of traditional theory building do. The difference is that we see the whole process as a two-way street. From a transactional perspective the understanding that teachers develop from all this reading and watching and listening is truly theirs, shaped as much by what they know as it is by what others know. Because their own experiences contribute to new understanding, their theory is applicable to their classrooms; and they establish their ownership of the theory as well. A transactional approach to theory building does not ask teachers to adopt another's theory but to create personal theory for themselves.

MOVING BEYOND PERSONAL THEORY

While it is important for teachers to have a strong personal theory we recognize that it is equally important for teachers to be able to share that theory with colleagues. It would be ludicrous to advocate that each teacher should remain content to possess and understand his or her personal theory without ever trying to see points of agreement with others. For our field to move forward we must share a theory base—an abstracted body of knowledge that is accepted in large measure by a group of teachers and researchers. We call this body of knowledge, these collective understandings, "collective theory."

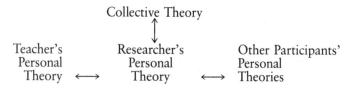

Figure 4.3
Model of collective theory.

This model does not imply that every teacher must share precisely the same collective theory. It simply means that a group of teachers might come together to share personal theories and discover or reach points of agreement through their transactions, as TAWL groups often do. Such a group could also be a grade-level team, the faculty of a whole school, the faculty in a particular content area, or the Board of Directors of the International Reading Association.

A group of first-grade teachers from Vermillion, South Dakota, spent a year doing that kind of collective theory building. After becoming familiar with the term "process writing" each teacher read the works of Lucy Calkins, listened to lectures from a university professor, and observed demonstration lessons from that professor in their own classrooms. As they became familiar with the whys and hows of process writing they began using some of the ideas they had heard about in their classrooms. Each teacher designed an inquiry project to answer a specific question about how process writing works in a first-grade classroom. Biweekly meetings to discuss data-gathering, insights, and conclusions provided the teachers with an opportunity to explicate their personal theories and to see points of agreement with their colleagues. Their own personal theories were strengthened and enriched through those ongoing transactions with one another.

This kind of shared theory, this collective theory is essential if teachers wish to discuss principles of instruction with one another. It is crucial if teachers wish to make generalizations about students, teaching, language, and learning. From a transactional view the development of collective theory is not driven primarily by published findings and theoretical statements but by the ongoing process of individual teachers making sense of their transactions with published writing, with their present and past experiences, and with each other.

At the beginning of the year, the first-grade teachers from Vermillion had talked about Lucy Calkins' approach to writing instruction; but by the end of the year they talked about their own personal views of writing instruction. One of the teachers in the group wrote this in her observation log at the end of the year:

> My own theory of writing is the way it is because of our interactions as a group, the way ideas can bounce around between us. It is also affected by our reading, and of course by my students.

Collective theory is grounded in data from authentic classroom contexts and mediated by the explicit personal theories of all those involved. The double-pointed arrows in Figure 4.3 indicate that all participants affect and are affected by these transactions, including the research and instructional context itself. The arrows also imply that this is an ever-changing process, a network of complex transactional events. As teachers grow, learn, research, and think, they change. As their personal theories change, our collective theories change and gain power.

SUMMARY

One major point of this book is that teachers can engage in research. We have pointed out that all teachers can also engage in theory building. We base this on our belief that all teachers operate from a theory base, even though we admit that many teachers' theories remain implicit. We have seen how becoming involved in research has helped us and other teachers to become more aware of theory's role in the classroom. Teachers who systematically gather data in their classrooms must deal with theoretical issues, if only to help answer their own questions. Teachers who choose to do research must be ready to deal with theoretical issues that come up when answering questions and moving through a quest.

The research of teachers is becoming increasingly important to the building of collective knowledge for the entire profession. No longer can language educators be content to wait for new knowledge, data, and insights to come only from university professors who have extensive research funds and strong research agendas. The third-grade teacher in the rural classroom can offer rich data and powerful insights to the profession, insights that can push our thinking and add to our knowledge base. No longer must teachers be content to defer to the "star system" of instructional research, a system in which classroom teachers wait to learn from the "true luminaries" of the profession. Each of us has something to contribute, and it is only as we come together to share our insights and our theoretical understandings that our evolving theories will benefit the children we want to touch.

5. What Joe Taught Me: A High-school Teacher Builds Theory

Leslie Patterson

I nervously looked from one tenured professor to the other. It was my entrance interview into the doctoral program at a large state university. Until now, the questions had been fairly easy.

"What is your theoretical approach to language arts instruction?"

Theoretical approach? But I teach high-school English. What should I know about theoretical approaches? That was what I had come to the university to be taught.

Since that day I have read journal articles and books; I have attended conferences and workshops; and I have taken and taught university courses. Goodman and Graves, Macrorie and Moffett, Shaughnessy and Smith are now familiar names. During part of that time I continued to face 100 twelfth-graders five days every week. Now, as a university teacher and researcher, I meet that many preservice teachers each semester.

At some point during those years I became a different kind of teacher. After many frustrating years of assigning and grading five-paragraph themes I made an amazing discovery. I discovered that before teachers can design effective instructional activities we must first understand something about the way people learn to read and write.

That's why the professor had asked me about theory. As a professional I am expected to have a research-based rationale for what I do in the classroom. That is an amazing realization—amazing because it took me years of teaching and graduate course work to discover something that should be obvious to the greenest novice.

I know now that the research base for language arts instruction is growing quickly, drawing on work in sociology, psychology, anthropology, linguistics, and literary and rhetorical theory. I have adopted and am continuing to learn about this interdisciplinary, sociopsycholinguistic approach to literacy learning. I agree with many researchers that language learning is a context-bound, transactional process in which individual learners use the graphophonemic, syntactic, and semantic systems of the language to create meaning. I also recognize that we have much more to learn about this complex process.

I gradually came to those realizations by listening, reading, and transacting with the specialists I know; but I was still slightly skeptical. For some reason I did not fully trust all those researchers and theory builders. I wanted to see it work in my classroom before I openly advocated it. After all, if we can't see theory work for our own students what good is it?

During the time I began to read that research I taught in a large suburban high school—tenth-, eleventh-, and twelfth-graders. These classes included students with a wide range of writing and reading abilities and attitudes, as well as different family and cultural backgrounds. As often as possible I chose learning activities endorsed by sociopsycholinguistic researchers—reading whole books, articles, and stories; and writing whole messages for real purposes. I avoided isolated spelling, vocabulary, and traditional grammar exercises. I admit that I began cautiously, but as I began seeing positive results—better rapport with students, fewer attitudinal problems, and longer, more interesting writing products—I gained self-confidence and used more and more of these activities.

I used what has come to be called a reading/writing workshop approach, with a great deal of informal and spontaneous conferencing and peer-editing. I was pleased to see college-bound students respond more thoughtfully and critically to the literature than had their peers in years past. I was even more pleased to see many of the low-achieving students more confident and enthusiastic in their reading and writing. The approach really worked. Apparently I did need that theoretical grounding.

I came to view myself as a researcher. I have also come to some conclusions about the way students learn language most efficiently and about how to help students connect what goes on in language arts class with students' reading and writing in the real world. Not so coincidentally my conclusions match four of the generalizations that sociopsycholinguistic researchers make about the language-learning process. Those generalizations, along with my findings that serve as support for them, are discussed below. For each of these students whose growth I describe I could cite many more who also benefited in similar ways.

LANGUAGE LEARNING IS FUNCTIONAL

Dennis, a typical basic student—an unenthusiastic and poor writer—illustrated the functionality of language learning for me. Although students first hear about paragraphing in the primary grades, sometimes the concept of "topic sentence plus support" is only rote learning until a student actually needs to organize his thoughts.

One morning, as I was checking the roll, Dennis had begun to answer a letter from his pen pal, another twelfth-grader in a different class. From his seat in the back row Dennis suddenly demanded, "I gotta know about paragraphs!" I stopped my roll-checking; the attendance office could wait. I asked him exactly what he needed to know about paragraphs. This twelfth-grader who had surely heard the answer dozens of times in this and previous English classes said rather impatiently, "Well, I need to know when you start a new paragraph!" In twelve years Dennis had not assimilated that concept, not until he needed it to communicate, not until it was functional for him.

LANGUAGE LEARNING IS SOCIAL

As Linda Crafton (1983) describes the social nature of language learning, she points out that the need to communicate is a prime motivator for language acquisition.

I saw many illustrations of this social aspect of language learning as my students wrote to pen pals. High-achieving students tried to help lower-level students build self-confidence and improve their skills. Native Texans eagerly wrote long letters to foreign students at a nearby university. Shy students teased their pen pals from the safety of their writing identities. The most impressive effect of this social function on the writing of the students was the increased length of students' letters compared to their expository assignments.

Robin, another basic student, began the year writing short, simple sentences in very brief paragraphs. During the year Robin chose a pen pal at a nearby university. She wrote enthusiastically to him, flirting with this mysterious older man. With the added social dimension Robin's fluency increased dramatically. One of her letters contained fifty-eight t-units, five times the number in her introductory letter to him and five times as long as most of her expository assignments. If all the writing assignments had incited this enthusiasm and fluency Robin's writing could have improved far more than it actually did with assignments that did not offer opportunities for authentic communication.

Certainly this social aspect of language learning is worth serious consideration by curriculum and instructional planners.

LANGUAGE LEARNING IS CONTEXT-BOUND

Pragmatics—or the choices concerning the message, medium, and audience—(Atwell, 1984) is another important sociopsycholinguistic concept for teachers. If students perceive instructional activity as a chance to send an authentic message to a real audience the pragmatic choices they make will have validity in the world outside the classroom. In more academic assignments the classroom itself becomes the authentic context and the teacher becomes the audience. Any learning that occurs is "merely academic." There is little chance that most students will transfer what they are learning beyond the classroom context.

Again, the use of letters seemed to be especially effective with the less confident and competent writers, probably because a letter provides an authentic context for the communication attempt: the situation; the purpose; and, most important, the audience. In addition to the pen-pal experience, I found that expository assignments couched in terms of a letter—to an editor, to a character in a book, to an author—were generally more successful than a more abstract expository assignment. In fact, my student teacher reported that Jimmy, another basic student, complained about an assignment to write a paragraph: "Why didn't you have us write a letter? I can write letters better than I can write paragraphs." Perhaps authentic contexts are, if not essential, at least helpful in fostering language learning.

LANGUAGE LEARNING IS TRANSACTIONAL

Many researchers have come to view the language-learning process as "transactional," meaning that all the elements come together as an organic whole, that each participant affects and is affected by all others. Harste, Woodward, and Burke (1984a) say that this view of language learning "assumes that meaning resides neither in the environment nor totally in the head of the language learner, but rather is the result of ongoing sign interpretation." This transactional view of language learning follows from and is dependent on the previous three, that language learning is functional, social, and context-bound.

I saw many examples of these transactions during my years of exploration into sociopsycholinguistic approaches to language learning. Probably the most dramatic example is that of Joe, another basic student, who had not responded to any class activities early in the year. He spent the first semester with his nose in a book of his own or with his head on his desk. He refused to participate in anything that did not interest him. His writing was legible, but hardly readable; his syntax merely reminded me of conventional English syntax. He failed the fall semester.

Then, in February, the students in Joe's class read a novel, and each one completed four of ten suggested writing activities. Joe did read most of the book and participated in class discussion—a definite improvement over his past record. One of the writing assignments he chose was a letter to the author of the novel. When Joe came up to show me his first draft of the letter I was pleasantly shocked. It was one-and-one-half pages long; it had only one sentence structure error, and three or four misspelled words. It was undoubtedly the best thing Joe had written all year. When I expressed my surprise and pleasure, Joe said, "Well, *this* is to an important author." After one or two revisions Joe mailed the letter. Steadily, Joe gained confidence with his writing. He participated more and more in class discussions; and he began turning in daily assignments.

By May, Joe had a "B" average. He had written a lively character analysis of Macbeth and his Lady; and he had interviewed class members for an informative paper on the effects of nuclear war. I noticed that Joe had begun to visit with the boys who stood next to him in the hall before school. Earlier, he had stood alone, almost sullenly.

One day, during his study hall, I invited Joe to join a college-bound class while they were writing satires. He chose to join a group with two good-looking, vivacious girls; and he laughed and talked with them throughout the period. Their group came up with as impressive a "modest proposal" as any of the other groups.

Finally, weeks later, Joe received a reply from his author—an autographed copy of the novel. Joe was thrilled; but he almost tore the mailing wrapper apart looking for a personal letter. Apparently, when Joe had begun using language to interact with real people he somehow became a different person.

Joe and I had come a long way together in a short time. Not long before Joe had been failing English. By the end of the year Joe was actually reaching for opportunities to read, write, speak, and listen to other human beings.

Not long before this I had simply met classes every day, frustrated by my students' lack of motivation and bored by their writing. After I met Joe and his classmates I began exploring the value of the sociopsycholinguistic approach to language instruction, learning from published researchers and from my own students. I have finally developed a research-based, theoretical approach to language arts instruction.

CONCLUSIONS AND IMPLICATIONS FOR RESEARCH

I add my voice to the chorus of those calling for more dialogue between university and public-school professionals. Although that is a perennial concern it seems to become more crucial each year, as the public demands accountability and excellence in teaching.

In many parts of the country legislators are mandating curriculum and instruction not based on our current knowledge of language learning. Parents and taxpayers base their expectations on what they see in the media and what they remember from their own schooling, both of which are necessarily incomplete and probably uninformed accounts of what is or should be happening in language arts classrooms.

Many university professors are knowledgeable and caring individuals who have the expertise to demonstrate effective instructional approaches, and many public-school teachers are desperate for ideas to help them deal with increasingly complex challenges. For some reason, though, we don't talk to one another very often. This lack of dialogue among language arts professionals often paralyzes us in the political arena, as well as in the area of instructional innovation.

I firmly believe that one avenue for this needed dialogue is cooperative research and "cooperative pedagogy" (Harste, Woodward, and Burke, 1984b). I am certainly not the first to call for cooperative research efforts between university and public-school people (Rich, 1984; Myers, 1985), but it cannot be emphasized too strongly nor too often. As university researchers ground their theory building in classroom realities and as teacher researchers build their theory bases everyone will profit—especially our young language learners.

III

PRODUCT: FINDINGS

6. Sharing Your Research Findings through Publication and Service

R. Kay Moss

Cindy Elliott had taught in a self-contained special education classroom for many years. Her move into a regular first-grade classroom came only after much careful thought. Yet with the encouragement of veteran first-grade teacher Nora Miller and others, Cindy made the switch. During Cindy's first year as a first-grade teacher she carefully selected and avidly read professional literature on literacy learning; watched her team teacher, Nora Miller, successfully use language experience, writing, big books, and choral reading; and began research in her classroom to identify the teaching strategies that were best for her own style of teaching.

That year Cindy also initiated a local TAWL group (Teachers Applying Whole Language), started a whole language special interest group in her state reading association, and began writing a column for other primary-grade teachers that is published in the state reading journal.

Why did Cindy Elliott need to share her developing personal theory about reading and her teaching strategies through these outlets? Cindy has a commitment to learning that helps her reach out to find some answers to her questions. She enrolled in a writing course at a nearby university to help her understand the writing process so that she can help her students with that process. By taking the writing course, and often writing with others, Cindy developed confidence as an author. She has also developed strong working relationships with her principal, other teachers, and other educators throughout the state who help guide her reading in the professional literature. Cindy is a professional and demonstrates this professionalism through her growth as a teacher and service to the profession. And, most importantly, Cindy is a questioning teacher who takes risks in the professional community. She is able to say, "Here is what I believe at this time."

WHY SHOULD WE SHARE RESEARCH FINDINGS?

Cindy's personal need to share her professional growth through publication and service is not unique to her. Teachers like Cindy often share their research findings with others. We need to do this because sharing findings brings a natural conclusion to a research project; opens new possibilities and new questions; and creates a sense of pride, accomplishment, and professionalism. We also need to share findings to help clarify our own thinking about research and our personal theories, help other teachers develop instructional theories, and help us all build collective theory.

To Help Teachers Build Theory

When we are actively engaged in finding answers we have the knowledge that will help other teachers develop theories in their classrooms. Only when we share our research findings can other teachers learn from those experiences.

As an example, meet Avril Font. Avril had always presented new vocabulary to her fourth-graders in the context of a sentence or a paragraph that she provided. The fourth-grade children were encouraged to say other words that meant about the same and fit into the sentence. But then Avril noticed that many of the meanings and connotations of these new words were being omitted in classroom discussions. To explore this problem she placed vocabulary words on the board in isolation, rather than using the words in teacher-generated sentences. After a few lessons Avril found that by presenting words in isolation she could draw multiple meanings from the children; no longer constrained by the context imposed by her sentences they provided a variety of contexts for the word. In Avril's unique classroom setting multiple meanings and connotations can be drawn from children and a richer understanding of stories can be achieved.

While Avril's findings through her classroom-based research are applicable in her classroom these findings may not be applicable in all settings or in all instances of learning the meanings of words. But by sharing her findings other teachers can begin to examine and investigate this teaching strategy in their classrooms.

To Clarify Personal Theory

In sharing the findings of teacher research we are compelled to outline, describe, and discuss elements from our inquiry. To do this, first we search through the data, think about what the data may mean, rethink what the data may mean, collaborate with others, and, finally, make some statements about the data. This process of stating the findings is similar to peer debriefing during the research process; however, it does more than help us determine results. It also helps us clarify our personal instructional theory.

Avril Font's personal theory about how language is learned is more well-defined after she did her classroom-based study. Rather than accept the notion that words are always best introduced in context, she now has a personal theory that pushes the traditional practice to include context the children themselves provide.

To Build Instructional Theory

Because teachers are always concerned with day-to-day instructional decision making, our research questions and the search for answers are pragmatic in nature. This is not to say that the research is somehow less theoretically based, less "worldly," or contributes less than other research to the total knowledge of the profession. Rather, just the opposite is true. Research that is classroom-based because of its ecological validity makes more significant contributions to our understanding of learners and learning within the context of classrooms than research that is not classroom-based. The research findings of teachers can help build more valid instructional theory for all of us, and eliminate the gap between what theoreticians are saying from "ivory towers" and what teachers are doing on the "front lines."

Teacher research must be shared with other teachers at local and national levels who are actively building instructional theory. As collaborators, educators from schools, universities, and administrative offices can build stronger theoretical models.

WHEN SHOULD WE SHARE THE RESEARCH WITH OTHERS?

A teacher involved in classroom-based research will never emerge from a laboratory and shout, "Eureka! I have it!" A classroom-based research project always involves time and the use of other people's ideas and perspectives. Throughout the study others are involved in peer debriefing, triangulation, and as participant and nonparticipant observers to validate and add trustworthiness to the study. So the question of when we share findings actually becomes, "When should we share findings with others outside of the immediate few who are involved in the study?"

Sharing with others will be helpful when:

1. we want to check with others about the data and for possible interpretations of the data.
2. we develop working hypotheses for the classroom and begin to implement changes. It may add perspective to our thoughts to share some preliminary findings with a principal or another teacher not previously involved with the study at this near-conclusion point. This may only mean mentioning some of the changes that will be made in our instructional strategies.
3. we wish to share working hypotheses and implications with the larger educational community. After implementing changes within the classroom, looking carefully at the data produced in the classroom, and clarifying what those data seem to say, those outside of the immediate context need to know what we have learned.
4. we want a chance to transact on paper with the data and the tentative findings that we have drawn.

WHAT IS PUBLISHING?

There's more than one joke about the motto "publish or perish" in higher education, but most K-12 teachers have not formally published and may be unaware of the many possible audiences and the procedures involved in addressing those audiences.

Publishing is making information known to others. This is done in a variety of ways, some formal and some informal. Formal publishing possibilities include dozens of educational journals at national, regional, or state levels; local and state newspapers, as well as districtwide newsletters; presentations at local workshops, inservice trainings, or conferences; and presentations to educational associations at state, regional, or national conferences.

Less formal means of publishing research can include presenting at parent-teacher meetings, teacher committee meetings, faculty meetings, or over coffee with another teacher. While a formally written research manuscript cannot be published in more than one educational journal, the findings themselves can and should be disseminated to as many people as is reasonably possible. Appendix D of this book lists the names and addresses of several associations that disseminate information about areas of educational specialty through journals and/or conferences.

The rest of this chapter outlines some information helpful when submitting a conference proposal or a manuscript for possible publication.

HOW DO I SUBMIT A CONFERENCE PROPOSAL?

Nearly every educational association has at least one annual conference. An annual conference is held at about the same time but in a different city each year. Most of the presentations at the conferences are given by teachers and others who are members of that association. Generally, though, conference presentations can be given by anyone who follows the guidelines for submitting a proposal and has it accepted.

Guidelines for Submitting a Proposal

Teachers wishing to present research findings at an educational conference should get in touch with the educational association with interests most similar to the research topic. The association will provide membership information, and when the call for program proposals is mailed, members will automatically receive this information. Proposals must be submitted many months before the actual conference takes place.

Before writing a proposal it is a good idea to read one that resulted in an invitation to present at an earlier conference. Another teacher or a university professor who has presented can often provide copies of proposals accepted in previous years (*see* Appendix E for a sample proposal).

Before writing the proposal researchers should have completed their studies or at least have the study at a point near enough to completion so they can provide all the necessary information requested on the form.

When writing the proposal researchers are asked to provide information such as the most suitable audience (K-12 teachers, supervisors, administrators, parents, university professors), the title of the presentation, the grade level(s) to which it relates, the format of the meeting (symposium, workshop, session, panel discussion, research report, and others), and an outline of the presentation. Occasionally a conference will have a particular theme that will be the focal point for many of the presentations. Some professionals feel that writing the proposal with this theme in mind might be helpful.

The body of the proposal provides information such as the objectives of the program, the content to be presented, and the methods of presenting content. Proposal writers must be very clear and concise when summarizing their research. The methodology of the research should be carefully explained and well-documented. Finally, the proposal should be neatly typed, proofread, and submitted prior to the deadline.

The procedure for selecting acceptable presentations takes several weeks, sometimes months. Proposals are blind reviewed (read without the submitters' names on them, which promotes fairness in the review process) by members of the association who are on the program committee.

When a proposal is accepted, invitations to present are sent to those who wrote the proposal. When rejected, a polite form letter is sent to the proposal writers informing them of the decision. Although submitters seldom receive specific feedback, often proposals are rejected because there are too many submitted for the specified grade level or audience, or because there are too many submitted on a closely related topic. Proposals are also rejected because there is too much content to cover in the allotted time, the proposal was poorly written, the research procedure was inadequate, the research was not completed, the conclusions drawn were inappropriate, or a number of related reasons.

Planning for a Conference Presentation

If a proposal is accepted, the writer has an obligation to present the research findings or, if necessary, have a colleague present them. Only in extreme circumstances would the teacher ever withdraw the program entry, and never without previously notifying the association or program committee. Being a "no-show" jeopardizes future appearances on the program.

Planning for the conference presentation takes much time and professional commitment from the teacher. The research must be presented in such a way that others will be able to construct working hypotheses for classrooms and develop more viable instructional theory from it.

Preparation for the presentation should include the following important considerations:

1. What are the interests, needs, and background knowledge of the audience?
2. What visual aids are needed for the most effective presentation? How can audiovisual aids be used to "show, not tell" the research findings? What media equipment is typically provided at the conference?
3. How can the content and delivery engage the audience?
4. What are the time constraints? How can the time be used most effectively?
5. How can handouts be used most effectively?

HOW DO I PUBLISH MY FINDINGS?

Publishing gives authors a sense of present and past and provides a record of achievements and a starting point for future writing endeavors (Graves, 1983). Writing for publication also helps authors clarify their thoughts, forcing them to be precise in both their thoughts about the research and the expression of those thoughts.

Journal Selection

The process of writing for publication begins with selecting the journal. It should be chosen after considering several criteria:

1. Who are the readers? Perhaps this is the most important question that an author should consider when writing for publication. The journal's editor will read the manuscript with the audience in mind; if the topic is not of interest to the audience, it will be rejected.
2. What is the journal's style? Many journals appreciate conversational, first-person manuscripts; others expect a style that is more formal.
3. What is the preferred length of the manuscript? Can the research be adequately explained in a manuscript of this length?

There are many resources available to help teachers answer these questions. Perhaps the best way to determine if a manuscript would be of potential interest to the journal is to examine several back issues of the journal. These can be requested from the journal's editor or often found at a university library. Many associations publish directories of international, national, state, and affiliate organizations that publish material of interest to their members. Each journal and the name and address of its current editor is listed in this directory. They are updated yearly and can offer a wealth of possible sources for publishing research.

Other potential sources include articles by Kenneth Henson (1984, 1986, 1988) that give details about many educational journals. Another information source about a particular journal is its editor. Editors can supply potential authors with a copy of the editorial policy, a call for manuscripts, and guidelines for authors.

Submitting the Manuscript

After writing the manuscript there are certain requirements for submitting it to a journal. These requirements differ from publication to publication but are explained either in the journal itself or in editorial guidelines for authors. Before submitting a manuscript the author must:

1. make sure the correct form for headings, subheadings, and references has been used. Many educational journals use the third edition of the *Publication Manual* of the American Psychological Association (1983) as the style manual, but teachers should also examine the journal itself for questions of style.
2. type the manuscript according to the guidelines. Do these specify certain margins and spacing?
3. carefully proofread the manuscript.
4. include the appropriate numbers of clear, clean copies; a self-addressed stamped envelope; a cover letter to the editor; and anything else required by individual editors (abstracts, loose postage, biographies).

The process for getting a manuscript in print generally takes several weeks or even months. First, the author will receive a card or letter saying that the manuscript has been received. The manuscript must be reviewed, either by professionals in that particular area of education or by the editorial staff. After the decision is made to publish the article editors may ask the author to make certain revisions (editorial changes, reduce the number of tables, etc.). Others will edit certain aspects of the article themselves (delete sexist language, etc.). As the final aspect of the research process making these finishing touches to an article that will soon be printed can provide the author with a sense of pride and completion, and offer the teacher a rewarding sense of professionalism that growing numbers of teachers are enjoying.

SUMMARY

As teacher researchers grow professionally, like Cindy Elliott, they often look for ways to reach beyond their own classrooms to share their findings. Conference presentations and publications offer teacher researchers a satisfying culmination to a study and a departure for future questions and quests.

7. What Natsumi Taught Me and What I Am Teaching Others

Terresa Payne Katt

As a classroom teacher in Spring Branch, a large mid-urban public-school district, I was part of a collaborative team charged with planning and implementing a developmentally appropriate prekindergarten program. As a team we worked hard to plan a program built on current research in early childhood education, and based on the widely accepted belief that young children need to manipulate, explore, and investigate the environment extensively so that learning can take place. As with any new program, though, it became clear during implementation that we had much to learn about four-year-olds.

Most of the questions that began to surface centered around young children's literacy learning, the area that I least understood. I also discovered very quickly that much of what I would learn in the next few years would come from the kids themselves. It didn't take me long to realize that they had much to teach their teacher.

As an undergraduate I had studied the works of Charles Read, Frank Smith, Ken Goodman, Yetta Goodman, Roach Van Allen, and other prominent researchers in the field of language arts instruction. As a result I was steadily building a whole language orientation to language arts throughout my undergraduate work. As I began my teaching career in a first-grade classroom my practice was built on this explicit theoretical orientation based on current research.

But as I moved from teaching first grade to prekindergarten, not all of my theory-based instruction made the transfer. Although I was still convinced of the power of language experience and predictable materials in support of early language learning, I also felt compelled to incorporate phonics, in isolation, as part of my program. After all, these were just four-year-olds. It seemed sensible then that little kids needed little pieces of language before they could read or write. Tradition implied that reading-readiness activities were about all four-year-olds could handle, so tradition became the driving force for my instruction.

I realize now that I just didn't know enough about natural literacy development. The growing frustration I felt about what I was doing in the classroom propelled me into a quest—a search for a better way to help my children to become literate. I had questions—lots of questions—about the "whats" and "hows" of natural literacy development for four-year-olds in school. The questions led me to my own classroom inquiry, and I began to view teaching as research.

As I observed kids in the classroom I suspected that they were much more capable and naturally curious about reading than I was allowing opportunities for in the classroom. Just what was reading instruction for these children, and when should it begin? Were four-year-olds "ready" for reading instruction when they entered my classroom? If they were, how would a teacher know? I was the teacher, and to be effective I needed answers. So my experience as a teacher researcher began with one broad, important question: "Should we teach four-year-old children to read as they begin formal education in school?"

As my quest for answers began, my question led me to the current literature. As I read the works of Goodman (1983); Harste, Woodward, and Burke (1984); Holdaway (1979); Newman (1984); and others, I began to see literacy learning for these four-year-olds in a totally new light. The research was abundant in support of a literacy program for young children when they begin formal schooling. I realized that young children growing up in a literate society already possess a great deal of language knowledge when they enter prekindergarten. The roots of literacy are growing strongly long before schools begin instruction, and so literacy development in school must be seen as an extension of natural development (Y. Goodman, 1983).

This research had an immediate, powerful impact on me. I realized that I had not only lowered my expectations for the children simply because of their ages, in effect narrowing their opportunities for learning, but had also restricted their written language learning to reading alone. What a shock it was for me to discover that four-year-olds could write, too! I was amazed at the written and oral language capabilities of four-year-olds that were documented in research; and it troubled me deeply that I had been so unaware of these findings. Realizing that my classroom practices no longer matched my theory caused me a great deal of grief and confusion.

But as soon as I discovered these things I began to develop a more appropriate program to help support the children's language learning, a program that would also reflect my whole language background and beliefs. What a relief! The classroom soon felt much more natural for these young children as I began to include both reading and writing, and introduced reading, writing, speaking, and listening activities, all organized around a weekly theme.

I soon started describing my classroom environment as "print rich," because there were now many more opportunities for transactions with print and a new emphasis on literature. There was no longer a place in that classroom for the "letter people" I had used in isolated phonics lessons.

Reviewing the literature had seemed to give me the "permission" I needed to challenge traditional practice in search of a better way to help young children become literate. Setting up my print-rich environment was the first step in building a successful program for four-year-old children.

In my "new" classroom many opportunities to read and write were an integral part of each child's experience. Books were read daily to children by other children. A wide variety of literature was available in the classroom library for them to use individually or in groups. Shared reading activities included both expository and narrative forms, and involved predicting, choral reading, and retelling. The writing activities included daily journal writing, voluntary sharing, and language experience dictations with parent volunteers transcribing the children's language into their own books, which they then read to each other. The writing center made materials available to children throughout the day. My classroom invited, if not begged, children to read and write. But this was not enough for me.

As I set up the print-rich environment I had looked to the literature to help me decide what I was supposed to do as the teacher in this whole language classroom. The literature seemed to support an entirely indirect, facilitative role, but I wasn't sure I "bought" this; just being a facilitator in this environment was simply not enough to make the classroom work as I felt it could. I began then to take a more critical look at the existing literature, and at my own idea of whole language teaching in my classroom. My initial question of whether four-year-olds should begin reading instruction when they enter school had become: "What is the teacher's role in providing literacy learning opportunities for young children as they begin their formal school experience?"

I had to look beyond the literature to the four-year-olds themselves for answers to this new question. So, to document the children's responses as I experimented with both direct and indirect teaching styles, and to test my own experience against published research, I collected this data: children's self-portraits six times through the year, weekly writing samples, student-made big books and individual books, language experience dictations and transcriptions, and my own log of observations of the children's language use and learning.

From each of these data sources I can cite dramatic evidence of growth in meaning-making through literacy and in control of the conventions of written language. This growth was far beyond what I had come to expect. The findings indicated that all the kids were benefiting from a whole language approach that included both direct and indirect teaching styles. The children had taught me some important components of a successful whole language classroom. Each component is essential to the success they enjoyed, and none would be as powerful in isolation as they were in combination.

First, the children taught me that their success in my classroom was largely a result of high expectations. When my practice was based on a more traditional view of how children learn language, I treated the child as a passive learner and approached literacy as a matter of mastering a hierarchy of specific skills, with the names, sounds, and formation of letters being an appropriate literacy curriculum for young children. I concentrated on teaching letters and sounds; that's what the children learned and that was about all they learned. I was, in fact, limiting their potential language learning through my teaching. But when I began to use whole, real texts—some taken from children's literature and some from their own writing—they began to form a basis for making sense of language. As I began to involve kids in real literacy events and to expect them to demonstrate language growth as they used it, they did just that. As I provided opportunities and encouraged them to make their own connections, they did that too.

I also took on a more direct instructional role. I asked questions of them and answered their questions continually, carefully constructing a framework to increase the possibility of their making these connections.

One such instance in the classroom was when Chase asked, as he pointed to one of our language experience charts, "Mrs. Katt, why is there a space here and here and here?" as he pointed to the spaces between the words. As I explained that the spaces let us know where a word starts and where it ends he exclaimed incredulously, "You mean this is a word, and this is a word, and this is a word?" as he pointed to separate words on our chart. The whole class got excited. It was time to teach the concept of a word directly, and I did.

Taylor said, "Oh, I get it! Lots of words make a story."

For days the kids delightedly showed off their new discovery, and enjoyed identifying many words in the context of stories. The concept of *word* made sense to them because they learned it within the context of meaningful text, their teacher's expectations for success, and some direction in the process.

As I developed a more direct role for myself the children continually discovered and began to internalize other concepts of print as they explored natural texts both individually and with the support of the group. As I watched the kids I learned that my intentional, direct teaching had become as much a necessary part of my classroom as our mutual expectations for success as language learners. Turning them loose to explore a print-rich environment would not have provided enough elaboration or explanation for them to become so independent. I had to teach my children how to support and respect each other as individuals, and that individual differences were expected and valued. I encouraged them to take risks, and their attempts, however unconventional, were seen as part of the natural pattern of growth; but I don't apologize for encouraging kids in their moves toward conventionality. Some kids were ready to make those moves and wanted answers to their questions about the conventions of language. They helped me learn to do a better job of judging whether to teach something directly or allow them to discover it. I had learned that whole language teachers need not be afraid to teach directly when kids' own explorations of language produce a "teachable moment."

My students also soon taught me that the print-rich environment and some direct teaching were not enough in themselves. I found myself constantly assessing their language use and learning, looking for every opportunity to focus on what a child already knew about print and the functions of print. I soon realized that a whole language classroom is not complete without an active, supportive teacher who is constantly involved in observing, transacting with, and analyzing children as they participate in the processes of reading and writing. This teacher uses the information gained on a daily basis to meet the growing and ever-changing needs of the children in the classroom. This, too, is a very direct, active role—so much for the idea that a whole language teacher merely sets up an environment and lets kids explore it unattended!

Language learning is social; and I came to realize that the environment I provided wouldn't have been as powerful if I hadn't encouraged the children to talk and share ideas continually as they transacted in it. I saw kids learn daily from each other as a result of visiting about their work.

Natsumi, the youngest child chronologically and developmentally, spoke only Japanese and understood very little English. She spent most of the first six weeks of school trying to discover the limits for her behavior in the classroom, throwing tantrums and refusing to participate in anything for more than a few seconds. I worked very hard to help Natsumi become a part of the group. The other children had to be taught to tolerate her behavior, while she was taught to control it. Eventually, as she watched other children engage in the literacy experiences of the classroom, Natsumi began to engage in similar behavior for short periods, and she seemed to gauge the appropriateness of her actions by the responses she received from her peers and myself. With our approval her periods of participation and attentiveness increased. Initially, Natsumi had abandoned her attempts to engage in literacy almost as soon as she began them, but as a result of direct support from me and from her peers in a literate environment she began to read and write for increasing lengths of time. As she became more successful her behavior improved markedly. Her written products became increasingly detailed and more conventional as she experimented with oral and written language over time.

Many teachers currently believe that the processes of language are learned in a sequential order, that kids must learn to listen before they speak, speak before they read, and read before they write. As I documented the growth of these children, however, they showed me that keeping language processes together is a critical aspect of the teacher's role. I am convinced that oral and written language develop concurrently and that each offers support for the other as kids use language. The evidence in my classroom suggests that kids do not separate language in order to use it.

Brooks couldn't have illustrated this point better when he told another child how to go about writing a book. He explained, "How I write books is from reading books. I remember what I have to write from the book. It's easy because the book tells you what to write."

Other evidence for this conclusion relates to the English as a Second Language (ESL) children. About one-third of the children in my classroom spoke only Japanese and understood very little English when they entered the program in September. However, because I didn't limit these children to learning only spoken English they learned to read and write English with the same variety of success as the native English-speaking children. Ayumi, for example, did not speak any English at the beginning of the year. But as she participated in the literacy events that included active reading and writing, she not only began to speak in complete English sentences but was writing and reading them. In a letter to her parents at the end of the year Ayumi wrote:

Dear Mom and Dad

ILRNDBOTBeYOSILRNDBOT
DINOSAURILRNDBBOTeNSCTOILRNDBOTHLRURINILRNDBOTRABTOILRND
RLNGOBOOKILRNDCATILRNDBOTBOOKILRNDBOTDOGILRNDBOTSIPE
ILRNDBOTMATBOCSOILRNDBOTBATTFLYILRNDBOTCATPLE
ILRNDBOTROCSOILRNDBOTSTOR

Ayumi

I couldn't believe my eyes. When I asked her to share what she had written, she didn't even hesitate as she read:

Dear Mom and Dad,

I learned about bears. I learned about
dinosaurs. I learned about insects. I learned about Halloween. I learned about rabbits. I learned
reading books. I learned cat. I learned about book. I learned about dog. I learned about sheep.
I learned about math boxes. I learned about butterfly. I learned about caterpillar. I learned about rocks. I learned about star.

Ayumi

Had my role been to help children develop oral language skills before moving on to other language processes I wouldn't have seen the incredible growth in these children, growth that offers strong evidence for providing opportunities for children to engage in all the language processes simultaneously.

As I worked with the children in my whole language classroom I came to see my role as much more active than some of the whole language literature would imply, as I often directed instruction in both formal and informal ways. I had an explicit plan to help foster each child's language growth in the most natural way I knew how, and I encouraged kids to take risks in new language situations based on what they already knew. But I didn't limit a child's learning to his or her discoveries; I shared with the rest of the class each exciting discovery and optimized their opportunities to learn from each other. My classroom was carefully organized to encourage literacy events that included the teacher as an active participant in the transaction, along with the learner and the environment.

I had once thought that my kids were discovering everything for themselves, so it was quite a shock to find out, in one of my first graduate reading courses, that I had been using my own modified versions of a number of teacher-directed comprehension strategies such as cloze, ReQuest, the DRTA, analogies, and graphic organizers, to name a few. For a while I almost felt like a traitor to my own beliefs. With the help of the kids in my classroom, though, I soon came to realize that in combination with other elements of the classroom environment these strategies had contributed much to their success.

Doing research in my classroom helped me better understand that learning takes place one child at a time. It helped me learn to plan based on individual growth, needs, and development in the process; to see kids' unconventional writing and reading as lessons about their language growth and development. I learned to analyze what some would see as "mistakes" or "regressions" to help guide my direct and indirect instruction.

Becoming a teacher researcher has also meant a great deal to me in other professional settings. Not long ago I submitted a proposal to the annual meeting of the National Reading Conference (NRC). It was accepted, and the next December I found myself sharing my findings with a small group of teachers and university researchers in Tucson, Arizona. Jerry Harste, a researcher and writer I have read extensively and greatly respect, was in my audience. It's hard to describe how important I felt as he listened to my findings and we talked, researcher to researcher, during the discussion that followed the presentations. Not long before I wouldn't have thought it possible.

It was not only possible, it opened up a whole new set of opportunities for me to continue to grow as an educator, opportunities that arose within eight months of my NRC presentation. As others heard about what I was doing, I was invited to several school districts and two universities to speak about natural literacy development in school and classroom research. I also received several invitations to speak to parents at local churches, to special interest groups in early childhood education, and most recently to join a team of teacher researchers from across the country to speak at the annual convention of the International Reading Association in Atlanta. What began as an attempt to answer questions for myself in my classroom has resulted in many opportunities to share information with other educators and parents in many different settings.

I was very fortunate to have both financial support and released time provided by my school district to help me make the most of these opportunities. Without this support many of the experiences I mentioned would not have been possible. The district recognized the importance of sharing this work with other groups, and I was able not only to share the findings with others but also to share the changes and challenges I faced as a teacher in the process of inquiry. From this process of sharing I learned just how much teachers need this kind of information so they can begin to accept change less painfully and see children's "mistakes" as a natural part of the teaching, researching, learning process.

One of the most exciting changes for me has been to share my findings within my own district through staff development courses and visitations. The staff development courses have provided a common knowledge base and background from which we can work collectively. Visitations to my classroom by different observers have also helped me to further clarify the teaching practices I've described. All of this has allowed teachers to form a network of support as a collective movement toward whole language classrooms takes place. It has provided an opportunity for teachers in our district to work things out together, share ideas and materials, ask and answer questions as each becomes a decision-maker in the process. Through the support of their colleagues many of the teachers I have worked with no longer view teaching as an isolated act. Through their collegial effort the needs of more students are being met, and increased learning is taking place.

The most exciting opportunity for me is yet to come. I have just been selected as the new Coordinator of Primary Instruction in our district, and this will give me the chance to devote more time to supporting teachers who are trying to make changes in their instruction to increase learning opportunities for kids. Change, as I have experienced it, is not always easy or painless. As a part of the supervisory team I'll work to help make these changes go as smoothly as possible.

Sometimes there were regressions. For instance, when I discovered that I needed to involve kids in writing I went back to teaching letters one at a time. They needed letters to write "real" stories, didn't they? But it only took a few days for me to realize that they were learning more letters when we talked about the letters in their big books than when I was teaching letters one by one. Once again, my "letter people" went back into the box; only this time they stayed there. The children, as my informants, have helped me examine many assumptions and led me to many new and better understandings about language learning for young children in school.

As a teacher researcher I no longer feel that simply relying on what the experts have found to be true is enough to support the decision-making process I face each day both philosophically and instructionally. Instead, I use the valuable information shared by these experts as one basis for formulating my own theory. I began by reading the literature and continued to read it as I watched kids engage in language use and learning in my classroom and reflected on my role as the teacher. As a result of this transactive process I began to change the way I looked at children, at myself, at the roles I played as a teacher, and at theory. I've learned that theory and practice can be comfortable together when each informs the other.

As a practitioner I feel I have a powerful contribution to make in understanding how kids learn best and why. It stands to reason that we who are in the classroom every day are in a perfect position to do just that. It also stands to reason that teachers need to be encouraged to work alongside other researchers in educational inquiry if we are to maximize the potential benefits of these efforts. Teachers, as well as other researchers, have something significant to contribute in understanding how kids learn best. All researchers must accept and value the active role of the public-school teacher in this process for the sake of the children's learning and for the sake of theory-building throughout the field.

Studying children has not only increased my effectiveness in the classroom but has also empowered me to continue to learn and to take control of my classroom. I believe that other teachers encouraged to participate in this process would also benefit greatly from the experience. As I studied kids and myself I found a new commitment to my beliefs and the way I practice them in school. I know more clearly what I believe; I have evidence to support my beliefs; and I am willing to act on them. But, you may ask, how much of a difference can just one whole language teacher researcher in just one whole language classroom realistically expect to make? Well, I've certainly made more of a difference than I ever realistically expected. Maybe you will too.

IV

POWER

8. Making a Difference: Teachers, Research, and Power

Terresa Katt's story told in Chapter 7 is powerful. It's the story of one teacher helping her students grow. Through research she developed confidence in her decisions and a voice for sharing her story with others. Through sharing she enlisted other voices in support of her teaching and research. Those voices first supported her as she became a better teacher; and now they support her as she helps others grow professionally. Her experience illustrates the power inherent in the teacher research process.

It is up to individual teachers to generate that power. University collaborators and central office administrators can provide support and can facilitate the process, but empowerment comes from within. It has always been a teacher's responsibility to make instructional decisions. Many teachers have accepted this responsibility and have also chosen to do research, which ultimately enfranchised them as powerful professionals. Some, like Nancie Atwell and Regie Routman, have gained international prominence. Others, like Terresa Katt, are just beginning to have an impact on the profession at large. As we consider the powerful teacher researchers we know, four characteristics seem to emerge as critical:

1. They have all taken ownership of their research.
2. They have chosen methodologies consistent with their instructional theory bases.
3. They have expected—and have received—support from their colleagues and communities.
4. Through their professional activities they have been able to touch the lives of students and colleagues beyond their classrooms.

TAKING OWNERSHIP OF THE RESEARCH PROCESS

Teachers whose research is this powerful take ownership of their studies. We know that students must take ownership of their reading and writing in order to become fully engaged in the language process, to find their own voices, and to become powerful language users whose messages touch others and make changes. It is the same with teachers and research. The most powerful findings and conclusions come from researchers who are fully engaged in the research process. Teachers with that kind of ownership, that kind of commitment to their research generate findings that also touch others and make changes. Those findings are affecting the thinking of the whole profession and are changing instructional decision making in real classrooms.

That doesn't mean a teacher can't collaborate on a research team but it does mean that choosing to collaborate must be up to the teacher. It means that the effort should exemplify true collaboration among peers. For years researchers from outside the classroom have looked on teachers as mere consumers of research or as people who granted access to research subjects. Sometimes the teacher's proper role was to listen to an expert tell them what the research meant for instruction. At other times the teacher was considered a variable to be controlled or manipulated during classroom experiments. The researching role is new to most teachers, and taking ownership will be difficult for some, just as choosing topics is difficult for some novice writers. But if teachers are to make critical contributions to the field of educational research they must ask questions, make their own methodological decisions, come to their own conclusions, and write their own reports. This does not mean that each researcher works in a vacuum but it does mean that group decisions are negotiated among equals. In the same way that novice writers can be shown alternatives for authoring choices, novice researchers can collaborate with more experienced researchers so that together they can consider the possible opportunities and come to productive decisions. It means that teachers will often be the principal investigators. It also means that teachers will own their findings to apply as they see fit; and it means that teachers will accept the responsibility for their research decisions.

MAKING METHODOLOGICAL CHOICES

Additionally, teachers who become powerful through their research endeavors generally are committed to an explicit theoretical rationale. This rationale drives both their teaching and their research. They choose instructional methods that match what they understand about how students learn language; and they choose research methods that neither violate those theoretical principles nor disrupt their students' learning. Perhaps an illustration would be helpful here. Whole language teachers believe that aspects of language cannot be isolated from one another or from the contexts in which they occur. Because of their theoretical orientation to language instruction these teachers wouldn't consider trying to teach students language by giving them word lists. Neither would they expect students to become literate by looking at pieces of language isolated from authentic communication contexts. In the same way naturalistic classroom researchers believe that the events they study cannot be reduced to distinct variables analyzed outside of authentic learning situations. They would not try to understand a research event by concentrating on isolated variables. They would continually check their findings against the environmental and situational contexts of the classroom.

Because the assumptions of whole language teachers and naturalistic researchers are theoretically compatible we typically see whole language teachers choosing naturalistic research methodologies. When considering the use of control groups or pre- and posttests these teachers typically decide that such procedures are not helpful in describing and documenting what happens in their classrooms. Teacher researchers who work from an alternative theoretical framework might find these procedures useful. Often, when teachers know that there are methodological alternatives that fit their theoretical rationales, they are much more willing to do research.

BUILDING A SUPPORT SYSTEM

Classroom research is a risky and demanding business. For that reason teacher researchers need supportive and honest responses from colleagues; and they also need administrative support. The empowered and empowering teacher researchers mentioned at the beginning of this chapter have all sought and, to some degree received, this kind of support.

There are at least three roles that colleagues can play as they assist in the research process. The first involves providing emotional support. Colleagues who are honest, supportive, and nonjudgmental about the mistakes teacher researchers make, about their best guesses and tentative conclusions provide an emotional safety net that makes risk-taking possible.

The second role is that of peer debriefer. That kind of support can come at any point in the research process. Colleagues can help generate research questions. They may offer advice about what kinds of data to collect or how best to answer a question. Support may come in the form of comments about the data collection or the data analysis. Certainly responding to written reports of the research is a valuable dimension of support.

The third role involves researchers who join forces within these research networks. Colleagues may choose to work on a common question; they may decide to pool data; they may co-author research reports; or they may present their findings as a research team. The teacher researchers' work we see in the professional literature suggests a wide range of these collaborative arrangements. Apparently there is no ideal model for collaboration among classroom teachers, administrators, and/or university researchers. Those models that involve all parties as equals in negotiating research decisions, however, allow everyone to enjoy ownership in the process, and thus yield richer and more powerful results.

After collegial support the second kind essential to teacher researchers is administrative assistance, which stems from the explicit recognition that research is a legitimate and vital part of teaching. That recognition translates into such necessary aids as released time, supplies and equipment, travel money, a place to work, and assistants. University researchers often take this kind of support for granted. A renowned researcher at a prestigious university, for example, may have hundreds of thousands of dollars in research funding; a small army of graduate assistants; computers; private office space away from distractions; and time to think, write, and reflect.

These things are certainly good to have, but even the most renowned researchers don't have them all the time; and they still do excellent research. What do they have that enables them to be successful? What are these key kinds of support that university researchers have and that teachers in schools often lack?

Expectations

At any university it is expected that a faculty member is able to do research. Even in colleges that don't require research for promotion and tenure, no one is surprised when a faculty member undertakes research. Teachers, though, are seldom expected to be able to do research, and the expectation that research is something beyond their abilities can be demoralizing. Part of building a support group may mean exposing other teachers, administrators, and university people to teachers' research abilities through sharing their work in professional publications and at research presentations. The support group may meet on a regular basis to discuss this work; or they may simply see their task as dissemination of the work to those involved in policy-making.

Part of the support comes from recognizing the benefits of teacher research. Though universities seldom question the practical worth of research done by professors, teachers are sometimes asked by their administrators to guarantee that their research will make some immediate, dramatic, quantifiable difference in student achievement or attitude—a guarantee that no researcher can give. Powerful teacher researchers know that while their research doesn't always make that kind of immediate difference it does make other contributions. Every teacher we know who has done research is stronger for it—whether in knowledge, curiosity, ability and willingness to explore ideas, effectiveness in helping students learn, or in some combination of these. Research has made a difference by enabling teachers to make a greater difference with students.

Collaboration with Colleagues

Researchers who want to make this difference also need their colleagues. In universities there are colleagues available to researchers—at least by phone if not in person. Other faculty members and graduate students are usually willing, if not eager, to talk through research plans, help analyze data, and react to drafts of a research report. In schools, especially in elementary schools, teachers often work in isolation and seldom get the chance to think and talk together about questions of mutual interest. Not many teachers we know ever get the chance to call a colleague at another location—except from their own telephones at home. Few university faculty members have to ask for such help—it can truly be taken for granted. For teachers in schools this is almost never the case.

The teacher researchers who are making powerful differences are part of a strong support group. The group may have begun as an instructional team whose members are potential collaborators for research activities, who look for other ways of giving teachers more access to one another in the course of regular school days.

Along with access to colleagues, time to work with them, as well as time to think and work alone, is critical for researchers. For the most part teachers are not in charge of their own time; their day is a series of events that must take place at specific times, and very little is left over for their use. But professors schedule their own time outside of class hours—they set their office hours and have input into the scheduling of committee meetings and all other aspects of their work. They are able to determine when and for how long they wish to work on research, and reschedule at least some of their other work accordingly. As a result even professors with the heaviest teaching and advising loads have more time that can be scheduled for research than elementary or secondary school teachers. It is easy to promise teachers the time they need to carry out research projects; but in reality teacher researchers generally spend their own time on nights, weekends, and vacations to do research tasks. Those who expect and hope that teachers will do research must find ways of providing additional planning periods during the day, days of released time during the year, instructional assistants, or even occasional sabbatical leave.

Equipment

The majority of university professors have access to the kinds of equipment that are fundamental to research activities—file cabinets and folders, computers, telephones, desks, conference rooms, and so on. Even in colleges with very limited budgets for these things, what is available is usually at hand, and professors are typically told who to ask for the items they need. Teachers often have trouble storing all the data they've gathered when their file cabinets are already filled to bursting, and they haven't been told how to requisition another cabinet or who will approve the request. When they realize that a computer could be helpful, they also often realize that their school system's computer facilities are across town in the central office. When a five-minute phone call could really help solve a research problem, teachers face waiting in line in the principal's office through most of a lunch break. And when they need a quiet place to talk with colleagues their choices are their classrooms, with no place to lay out data for examination, and in the primary grades only one chair suitable for an adult; or the lounge, crowded with other teachers chatting over coffee or running the duplicating machine.

Supporters of teachers' research efforts can help by realizing that when teachers are truly respected as professionals and their research is seen as important and useful, ways will be found, even when budgets are tight, to increase access to the supplies and equipment these researchers need. Even in these nuts-and-bolts ways support for classroom researchers begins with respect.

INFLUENCE BEYOND THE CLASSROOM

Although teacher researchers can become powerful professionals they are often unassuming in their power. They may even be unaware that they have it; but daily those teachers are emulated by others. They are held up as examples by their administrators; and they are consulted by university colleagues. Theirs are the voices to whom legislators and publishers listen; and theirs are the voices that speak most convincingly to taxpayers.

Like all good teachers these people understand their special roles in children's lives; and they take that responsibility seriously. They continue to learn from their students and from colleagues; they take the risks inherent in instructional decision making; and they can explain their rationales to students, to parents, and to other professionals.

But many teacher researchers are more than simply "good teachers." Many of them have begun focusing on issues outside their classrooms. They have begun to share their knowledge with others. They are generally active in some movement toward instructional change: staff development, curriculum development, or policy-making at the district level and beyond. Perhaps these individuals would be powerful without doing research, but the inquiry process itself, as well as their data and findings, all play a major role in the professional growth of these teachers.

Within their classrooms they are thoughtful and informed decision-makers. Outside their classrooms they are articulate and informed advocates for children and for the contexts that support learning. Through their thoughtful inquiry in the classroom they have developed a level of professional self-respect that demands and deserves the respect of others, both inside and outside the profession. Terresa Katt's is the voice of such a teacher researcher.

SUMMARY

The role these powerful teacher researchers can play in both professional and political arenas should be obvious. If they obtain the support of their colleagues and their administrators, if they are provided with the time to participate in professional circles outside their classrooms, if they are somehow rewarded for their commitment and energy, if they get the professional respect they deserve, they can and will participate in changing policy and in staff development efforts that can ultimately alter the way we see schools and classrooms. Their input can help improve the ways we go about helping students learn.

Karen Smith and her colleagues at Herrera Elementary School in Phoenix, Arizona, used data from their classrooms to influence district policy decisions not to require basal texts. Carol Santa and her colleagues in Kalispell, Montana, used data from their classrooms to develop and validate the Content Reading Including Study Skills Project (CRISS), a content area reading and writing staff development model that has been a part of the National Diffusion Network since 1985. Marianne Mohr and her colleagues in Fairfax County, Virginia, wrote a book, *Working Together* (1987), explaining their approach to classroom research; and others in the same school district currently publish a newsletter about teacher research. The list could go on.

Teachers bring a unique perspective to educational problem solving, and teacher researchers bring a theory base and classroom data to support their unique perspectives. Theirs are strong voices which have not traditionally been consulted as educational policies were formulated. Perhaps that will change in the future. Perhaps, as more and more teachers begin doing research in their classrooms, more of them will speak up and help the profession make the best decisions possible, given our current knowledge of students and learning. Perhaps the profession will begin to ask teachers to describe "the state of the art." That's when teachers will finally be able to make a difference beyond their own classroom doors.

Today's researching teachers may find their quests taking them into the political arena to influence policies that affect our communities, our schools, and our students. They may find their quests taking them into graduate programs that ultimately offer other opportunities for research and service. Or their quests may help them discover new ways to touch their students' lives. Almost certainly these quests will help them build collaborative relationships with other questing teachers.

We have always heard that knowledge is power, but we aren't sure we really believe that. We think the real power lies in the questions we ask and in the quests we follow.

References

American Psychological Association. (1983). *Publication manual,* 3rd ed. Washington, D.C.: APA.

Branscombe, A. (1987). "I gave my classroom away," in *Reclaiming the classroom: Teacher research as an agency for change.* D. Goswami and P. Stillman, eds. Upper Montclair, N.J.: Boynton/Cook.

Calkins, L. M. (1985). "Forming research communities among naturalistic researchers," in B. W. McClelland and T. R. Donovan, eds. *Perspectives on research and scholarship in composition.* N.Y.: MLA.

———. (1986). *The art of teaching writing.* Portsmouth, N.H.: Heinemann.

Carnicelli, T. A. (1980). "The writing conference: A one-to-one conversation," in T. R. Donovan and B. W. McClelland, eds. *Eight approaches to teaching composition.* Urbana, Ill.: National Council of Teachers of English.

Crafton, L. K. (1983). "Oral and written language: Related processes of a sociopsycholinguistic nature," in U. H. Hardt, ed. *Teaching reading with the other language arts.* Newark, DE.: International Reading Association.

Dewey, J. (1929). *Sources of a science of education.* N.Y.: Horace Liveright.

———, and A. F. Bentley. (1949). *Knowing and the known.* Boston, MA.: Beacon Hill.

Donaldson, M. (1978). *Children's minds.* N.Y.: Norton.

Elbow, P. (1981). *Writing with power.* London: Oxford University Press.

Elsasser, N., and V. P. John-Steiner. "An interactionist approach to advancing literacy." *Harvard Educational Review.* 47, 355–369.

Emig, J. (1971). *The composing processes of twelfth graders.* Urbana, IL: National Council of Teachers of English.

Estes, T., and J. Vaughan. (1985). *Reading and thinking in the content classroom,* 2nd ed. Boston, MA.: Allyn and Bacon.

Genishi, D. (1984). "Research currents: What is a context for learning through language?" *Language Arts.* 61, 52–58.

Goodman, K., and Y. Goodman. (1976). "Learning to read is natural." Paper presented at the Conference on Theory and Practice of Beginning Reading Instruction, Pittsburgh, PA.

Goodman, Y. (1983). "The roots of literacy." Paper presented at the Annual Meeting of the National Reading Conference, Austin, TX.

Graves, D. (1973). "Children's writing: Research directions and hypotheses based upon an examination of the writing processes of seven-year-old children." Unpublished dissertation, State University of New York at Buffalo.

————. (1983). *Writing: Teachers and children at work*. Portsmouth, N.H.: Heinemann.

Green, J., and C. Emihovich. (1987). "Multiple perspectives analysis: Directions and issues." Paper presented at the 37th Annual Meeting of the National Reading Conference, St. Petersburg, FL.

Guba, E. G., and Y. S. Lincoln. (1981). *Effective evaluation: Improving the usefulness of evaluation results through responsive and naturalistic approaches.* San Francisco, CA.: Jossey-Bass.

Hairston, M. (1982). "Thomas Kuhn and the revolution in the teaching of writing." *College Composition and Communication. 33,* 91–105.

Halliday, M. L. K. (1975). *Learning how to mean.* London: Edward Arnold.

Harste, J., V. A. Woodward, and C. Burke. (1984a). "Examining our assumptions: A transactional view of literacy and learning." *Research in the Teaching of English. 18,* 84–108.

————. (1984b). *Language stories and literacy lessons*. Portsmouth, N.H.: Heinemann Educational.

Heath, S. B. (1983a). *Ways with words: Language, life, and work in communities and classrooms.* Cambridge, G.B.: Cambridge University Press.

Henson, K. T. (1988). "Writing for education journals." *Phi Delta Kappan. 69,* 752–754.

————. (1984). "Writing for professional publication." *Phi Delta Kappan. 65,* 635–637.

————. (1986). "Writing for publication: Playing to win." *Phi Delta Kappan. 67,* 602–604.

Holdaway, D. (1979). *The foundations of literacy.* Sidney, Australia: Ashton Scholastic.

Hunt, K. W. (1965). *Grammatical structures written at three grade levels.* Urbana, IL. National Council of Teachers of English.

Lee, S. C. (1987). "Teachers' perceptions of the process and function of theories of language learning." Doctoral dissertation, Texas A & M University, College Station, TX.

————, and L. A. Patterson. (1988). "The nature of transactional theory: Not static, but dynamic." Unpublished paper.

Lightfoot, S. L. (1983). *The good high school.* N.Y.: Basic.

McConaghy, J. (1986). "On becoming teacher experts: Research as a way of knowing." *Language Arts. 63,* 724–728.

Macrorie, K. (1980). *Telling writing.* Rochelle Park, N.J.: Hayden.

Meyers, M. (1985). *The teacher researcher: How to study writing in the classroom.* Urbana, IL.: National Council of Teachers of English.

Moffett, J. (1968). *Teaching the universe of discourse.* Boston, MA.: Houghton Mifflin.

———, and B. J. Wagner. (1983). *Student-centered language arts and reading, K-13: A handbook for teachers.* Boston, MA.: Houghton Mifflin.

Mohr, M., and M. Maclean. (1987). *Working together: A guide for teacher researchers.* Urbana, IL.: National Council of Teachers of English.

Newman, J. (1983). *The craft of children's writing.* Portsmouth, N.H.: Heinemann.

Patterson, L. A. (1985). "Becoming a teacher researcher: Another avenue to excellence." *English Journal.* 74(7), 98–102.

———. (1986). "The impact of theory-based instruction in a high school English classroom, in P. L. Anders, ed. *Research on reading in secondary schools.* Tucson, AZ.: University of Arizona.

———. (1987). "Responses to socio-psycholinguistic composition instruction in a secondary classroom: Toward a transactional stance for teacher researchers." Doctoral dissertation, Texas A & M University, College Station, TX.

Rich, S. (1984). "On becoming teacher experts: Classroom research as professional development." *Language Arts.* 61, 59–65.

Rogers, V. (1984). "Qualitative research—another way of knowing," in P. Hosford, ed. *Using what we know about teaching.* Alexandria, VA.: Association for Supervision and Curriculum Development.

Rosenblatt, L. (1978). *The reader, the text, the poem.* Carbondale, IL.: Southern Illinois University Press.

———. (1985). "Viewpoints: Transaction versus interaction—a terminological rescue operation." *Research in the Teaching of English.* 19, 96–107.

Sears, P. (1979). "Letter writing: A technique for treating writer's block." Paper presented at the annual meeting of the Conference on College Composition and Communication, Minneapolis, MN.

Shanklin, N. (1982) "Relating reading and writing: Developing a transactional theory of the writing process." Monograph in Language and Reading Studies, Number 3. Bloomington, IN.: University of Indiana School of Education.

Smith, F. (1971). "Twelve easy ways to make learning to read difficult and one difficult way to make it easy," in F. Smith, ed. *Psycholinguistics and reading.* N.Y.: Holt, Rinehart and Winston, 183–196.

———. (1975). *Comprehension and learning: A conceptual framework for teachers.* N.Y.: Holt, Rinehart and Winston.

———. (1983). *Essays into literacy.* Portsmouth, N.H.: Heinemann Educational.

Staton, J. (1983). "Thinking together: Language interaction in children's reasoning" in *The talking and writing series K-12: Successful classroom practices.* Washington, D.C.: Dingle.

Stezel, N. (1983). "Large scale writing assessment and writing apprehension." Illinois State Board of Education.

Vygotsky, L. (1986). *Thought and language.* Cambridge, MA.: MIT Press.

Appendices

Appendix A. A Graduate Course on Teacher Research: Syllabus and Bibliography

In 1988 John Stansell developed the first course on classroom research to be offered by Texas A & M University. We offer the syllabus and bibliography from that course as a possible framework for groups that wish to explore classroom research over a period of time.

Each discussion topic listed in the course calendar has a set of readings; the bibliography includes all of the readings mentioned in the calendar and a number of others. These are articles and books that the authors have found to be useful; there are certainly others and we encourage you to consider them as well.

The syllabus also describes course requirements: a position paper, a weekly log of reactions to readings and discussion, weekly summaries and reactions to readings for a partner's response, and a proposal for classroom research. While they are obviously not "requirements" in this context these activities may be useful ways to explore, plan, and reflect on research in your classroom.

In offering this framework we also encourage you to make changes as needed: rearrange the sequence of topics, add or delete topics, find other readings, modify activities, and vary the amount of time devoted to particular matters according to the experiences and needs of your group.

EDCI 689
Special Topics in Teacher Research
Spring 1989

John C. Stansell
Hours: MW 2–4

What is teacher research anyway? Just the newest fad? Another form of staff development? Could it be a major source of sound theory? A natural link of theory and practice? A means of sustainable growth for the whole profession?

Is it "real" research, taken seriously by established researchers? Do teachers really benefit from it? How can they find the time to do it? Since teachers aren't usually trained to do research, how can they learn how? Can any teacher do it? Should they? How do other teachers feel about their colleagues as researchers?

What does "collaboration" between teachers and university staff really mean? What does it involve? In these collaborative studies, who's in charge? What roles do/should teachers and university people play?

A growing number of teachers in the U.S., Canada, Great Britain, Australia, and elsewhere are conducting research in their classrooms. Many more teachers are interested in finding out what classroom research involves and how they might do some. As more and more teachers conduct their own research, and as more graduate students and professors join forces with them as collaborators, these questions and a host of others like them have arisen.

This course is intended for teachers interested in conducting research, full-time graduate students interested in collaborative research with classroom teachers, and anyone who is interested in exploring the issues and questions raised by this growing international movement.

Objectives

Participants in EDCI 689 will:

1. Become more familiar with the foundations, purposes, methods, procedures, and results of research by teachers.

2. Examine the potential contributions of this research to theory development as well as to practice.
3. Identify and examine issues and problems involved in teacher research, especially those surrounding collaboration among teachers and university researchers.
4. Develop and present a proposal for research that involves one or more teachers as principal investigator(s), and that may involve university researchers as collaborators.

Requirements, Guidelines, and Due Dates

1. Regular participation, in collaboration with a partner, in class discussions based on readings; weekly journal entries describing responses to discussions, readings, etc.
2. Position paper addressing a problem or issue related to teacher research or collaborative research. Describe the problem or issue thoroughly and clearly, critically analyze its several aspects or "sides," present and justify your position and recommendations.

   Incorporate readings from the attached bibliography, or elsewhere, as appropriate.

   Prepare the paper for submission to a professional journal (length about 10–15 double-spaced pages); several examples of manuscript form will be provided. Work with your partner in all aspects of this assignment.
3. Weekly one-page reviews of readings assigned/distributed in class. Reviews include a brief summary, statement of issue(s) identified by the reader, and a response to the issue(s). Partners will react to each other's reviews in class.
4. Research proposal involving one or more teacher researchers as principal investigators, which may include university researchers as collaborators. Proposals for collaborative studies must describe and justify, in the written proposal and/or the oral presentation, the exact roles intended for each party.

   Work with your partner in developing proposals; graduate students developing actual thesis/dissertation/record of study proposals should also work closely with their major professors on this assignment, and invite her/him to the oral presentation.

   The oral presentation will include a summary of each section of the proposal, during which class members' questions will address theoretical, methodological, and other issues as they arise.

   One week prior to the oral presentation, submit your written proposal in draft form to members of the class for review.

Course Calendar

Date	Topics, Readings
Jan. 19	Introductions

Jan. 19 — Introductions

Is this "teacher research" stuff just a new fad? A historical overview.

Jan. 26 — What kind of research is it? What do teacher researchers do? Procedures in teacher research.

Read Atwell, 1982; Clay, 1982; McConaghy, 1986; Ray, 1987.

Feb. 2 — Is it "real" research? Could you do it for a PhD? Research paradigms and teacher research.

Read Berthoff, 1981; Britton, 1983; Cook, 1984; Dewey, 1929; Dewey and Bentley, 1949; Goswami, 1984; Hodgkinson, 1957; Patterson, 1987; Patterson and Stansell, 1987; Rosenblatt, 1978, 1985; Stenhouse, 1981.

Feb. 9 — What's so great about it? Why do teachers do it? Why are professors and graduate students excited about it? Purposes and potentials of teacher research; teacher research and theory development.

Read Atwell, 1986; Berthoff, 1981; Bissex and Bullock, 1987; Corey, 1952; DeFord, 1985; Harste, 1985; Harste and Burke, 1977; Lee, 1987; McConaghy, 1986; Mitchell, 1980; Mohr, 1985; Patterson, 1987; Ray, 1987; Stansell and Patterson, 1987; Stenhouse, 1985.

Feb. 16 — How do you get started? And how do you gather data? Asking and refining research questions; using research literature as well as experience to develop questions; selecting data contexts and sources.

Read Atwell, 1986; Calkins, 1985.

Feb. 23 — How do you analyze this data? Isn't there a lot of it? Methods and procedures for data analysis.

Read Allen, *et al.*, 1988; Atwell, 1982, 1986; Myers, 1985; Stenhouse, 1975.

Mar. 2 — How can you make sure it's any good? And then, how do you decide what it all means? Quality control methods; drawing, applying, and generalizing conclusions in teacher research; theory building revisited.

Read Calkins, 1985; Goswami, 1984; Lee, 1987; Lee and Patterson (unpublished); Stansell and Patterson, 1987.

Mar. 9 — Then what? How do you share teacher research? When you finish a study, where do you go from there? Writing articles and conference proposals; giving presentations; editors, rejected manuscripts and proposals, and other headaches; your next (gulp!) study???

	Read Atwell, 1982; Goswami and Stillman, 1987; Mc-Conaghy, 1986; Mohr and McLean, 1987; Ray, 1987.
Mar. 23	I could stand some help, but who are the potential collaborators? Other teachers? My principal? The kids? The ins and outs of collaborative teacher research.
	Read Boomer, 1985; Bissex and Bullock, 1987; Buckley, 1987; Calkins, 1985; Mohr, 1985, 1987; Mohr and McLean, 1987; Patterson and Stansell, 1987.
Mar. 30	Should you collaborate with a university researcher? What are the ins and outs of that? Collaboration models and roles; "what to do when the collaborator comes"; the TAMU School/University Research Collaborative and the Teacher-as-Researcher Subcommittee.
	Read Allen and Albert, 1987; Applebee, 1987; Fox and Faver, 1984; Patterson and Stansell, 1987; Torney-Purta, 1985.
Apr. 6	Can we talk about this? Issues and problems in teacher research and collaboration.
	Read proposals, as assigned.
	Position papers due.
Apr. 13, 20, 27	Proposal presentations; read proposals, as assigned.
May 4	Course summary, evaluation; proposals due.

Bibliography

Recent Research by Teachers

Abbott, S. (1989). "Talking it out: A prewriting tool." *English Journal.* 78(4), 49–50.

Afflerbach, P., L. Bass, D. Hoo, S. Smith, L. Weiss, and L. Williams. (1988). "Preservice teachers use think-aloud protocols to study writing." *Language Arts.* 65, 693–701.

Austin, P. (1989). "Brian's story: Implications for learning through dialogue." *Language Arts.* 66, 184–190.

Bissex, G., and R. Bullock. (1987). *Seeing for ourselves: Case study research by teachers of writing.* Portsmouth, N.H.: Heinemann.

Bracale, E. M. G. (1988). "Signs of development: Busting through assumptions." *Language Arts.* 65, 658–660.

Buckley, R. (1987). "A funny thing happened on the way to reading readiness: A teacher learns from the learners. *Language Arts.* 64, 743–747.

Burk, J. (1989). "A study of the development of reading theory by preservice teachers." Doctoral dissertation, Texas A & M University, College Station, TX.

Burris, G. (1987). "Student as decision maker: The power of the reading-writing model." Paper presented at the thirty-seventh annual meeting of the National Reading Conference, St. Petersburg, FL.

Burton, F. R. (1986). "Research currents: A teacher's conception of the action research process." *Language Arts. 63,* 718–723.

Carlson, J. (1988). "Readers responding to 'Rappacini's Daughter.'" *English Journal. 77*(1), 49–53.

Carnes, E. J. (1988). "Teaching content area reading through nonfiction book writing." *Journal of Reading. 31,* 354–360.

Cordeiro, P. (1988). "Playing with infinity in sixth grade." *Language Arts. 65,* 557–566.

Docherty, M. (1988). "Teacher inquiry in the classroom: 'I don't know what's so exciting about me except my story.'" *Language Arts. 65,* 482–487.

Dorsey, D. (1987). "Teacher as decision maker: The power of the reading-writing model." Paper presented at the thirty-seventh annual meeting of the National Reading Conference, St. Petersburg, FL.

Everett, E. (1988). "At-risk first graders' responses to a reading/writing workshop." Paper presented at the thirty-eighth annual meeting of the National Reading Conference, Tucson, AZ.

Feldhaus, M. J. (1989). "Learning to teach children to read: A journey of discovery." *Reading: Exploration and Discovery. 11*(2), 34–37.

Forester, A. D. (1988). "Learning to read and write at 26." *Journal of Reading. 31,* 604–613.

Fowls, D. (1987). "Empowering students' meaning making and the effects of the reading-writing model." Paper presented at the thirty-seventh annual meeting of the National Reading Conference, St. Petersburg, FL.

Hess, M. L. (1989). "All about hawks or Oliver's disaster: From facts to narrative." *Language Arts. 66,* 304–308.

Johnston, P. (1989). "A scenic view of reading." *Language Arts. 66,* 160–170.

Kaisen, J. (1987). "SSR/booktime: Kindergarten and 1st grade sustained silent reading." *Reading Teacher. 40,* 532–536.

Katt, T. P. (1988). "Four year olds' response to a print-rich environment." Paper presented at the thirty-eighth annual meeting of the National Reading Conference, Tucson, AZ.

Knowles, J. G. (1988). "A beginning teacher's experience: Reflections on becoming a teacher." *Language Arts. 65,* 702–712.

Lindquist, D. B. (1988). "Joining the literacy club." *Reading Teacher. 41,* 676–680.

Manion, B. B. (1988). "Writing workshop in junior high school: It's worth the time." *Journal of Reading. 32,* 154–157.

McGuire, B. S. (1988). "Self-awareness: Toward greater control for young writers." *English Journal. 77*(2), 34–36.

Minns, H. (1988). "Teacher inquiry in the classroom: Read it to me now!. *Language Arts. 65,* 403–409.

Morningstar, C., and E. McKvoy. (1987). "Teacher as researcher: The use and interpretation of instructional strategies." Paper presented at the thirty-seventh annual meeting of the National Reading Conference, St. Petersburg, FL.

Myers, J., W. Serebrin, C. Beverstock, B. Smitten, and P. Bowman. (1988). "The sense preservice teachers make of the language arts/reading methods classes and field placement experience." Paper presented at the thirty-eighth annual meeting of the National Reading Conference, Tucson, AZ.

O'Keefe, T. (1988). "Exploring the role of reflection in literacy learning." Paper presented at the thirty-eighth annual meeting of the National Reading Conference, Tucson, AZ.

Patterson, L. A. (1987). "Responses to socio-psycholinguistic composition instruction in a secondary classroom: Toward a transactional stance for teacher researchers." Doctoral dissertation, Texas A & M University, College Station, TX.

Sanford, B. (1988). "Writing reflectively." *Language Arts. 65,* 652–657.

Saul, E. W. (1989). "'What did Leo feed the turtle?' and other non-literary questions." *Language Arts. 66,* 295–303.

Schaars, M. J. (1988). "Teaching *My Antonia,* with guidance from Rosenblatt." *English Journal. 77*(1), 54–58.

Smith, S. (1989). "To confer or not to confer: Children decide." *Teachers Networking: The Whole Language Newsletter. 9*(3), 6.

Sultan, G. (1988). "No more sixes, nines, and red lines: Peer groups and revision." *English Journal. 77*(5), 65–68.

Swoger, P. A. (1989). "Scott's gift." *English Journal. 78*(3), 61–65.

Trachtenburg, P., and A. Ferrugia. (1989). "Big books from little voices: Reaching high risk beginning readers." *Reading Teacher. 42,* 284–289.

Ziegler, A. (1989). "Questions children ask about texts." *Teachers Networking: The Whole Language Newsletter. 9*(3), 7.

Collaborative Research

Allen, K., and M. Albert. (1987). "Asking questions together: A researcher-teacher collaboration." *Language Arts. 64,* 722–726.

Erickson, F. (1989). "Research currents: Learning and collaboration in teaching." *Language Arts. 66,* 430–441.

Fox, M. F., and C. A. Faver. (1984). "Independence and cooperation in research: The motivations and costs of collaboration." *Journal of Higher Education. 55,* 347–359.

Phillips, D. C. (1980). "What do the researchers and the practitioner have to offer each other?" *Educational Researcher. 17*–20, 24.

Schwartz, J. (1988). "The drudgery and the discovery: Students as research partners." *English Journal. 77*(2), 37–40.

Torney-Purta, J. (1985). "Linking faculties of education with classroom teachers through collaborative research." *The Journal of Educational Thought.* *19*, 71–77.

Historical Perspectives on Classroom Research

Blum, F. H. (1955). "Action research—A scientific approach?" *Philosophy of Science.* 22, 1–7.
Buckingham, B. R. (1926). *Research for teachers.* N.Y.: Silver Burdett.
Cook, S. W. (1984). "Action research: Its origins and early application." Paper presented at the ninety-second annual meeting of the American Psychological Association, Toronto, Canada.
Corey, S. M. (1952). "Educational research and the solution of practical problems." *Educational Leadership.* 9, 478–484.
———. (1953). *Action research to improve school practices.* N.Y.: Horace Mann-Lincoln Institute for School Experimentation, Teachers College, Columbia University, New York, N.Y.
Dewey, J. (1929). *Sources of a science of education.* N.Y.: Horace Liveright.
Foshay, A. W. (1950). "Experimentation moves into the classroom." *Teachers College Record.* 51, 353–359.
———. (1955). "Action research as imaginative hindsight." *Educational Research Bulletin.* 34, 169–171.
Hodgkinson, H. L. (1957). "Action research: A critique." *The Journal of Educational Sociology.* 31, 137–153.
Lehmann, I. J., and W. A. Mehrens, eds. (1971). *Educational research: Readings in focus.* N.Y.: Holt, Rinehart and Winston.
Rapoport, R. N. (1970). "Three dilemmas in action research." *Human Relations.* 23, 499–513.
Wallace, M. (1987). "A historical review of action research: Some implications for the education of teachers in their managerial role." *Journal of Education for Teaching.* 13, 97–115.
Wann, K. D. (1953). "Action research in schools." *Review of Educational Research.* 23, 337–345.

Classroom Teachers as Researchers

Aber, J. (1988). "Composition teachers need to become teacher researchers: Reflections based on an ethnography of teacher training sessions." Paper presented at the annual meeting of the Conference on College Composition and Communication, St. Louis, MO.
Allen, J., J. Combs, M. Hendricks, P. Nash, and S. Wilson. (1988). "Studying change: Teachers who become researchers." *Language Arts.* 65, 379–387.
Anzul, M., and M. Ely. (1988). "Halls of mirrors: The introduction of the reflective mode." *Language Arts.* 65, 675–687.

Applebee, A. N. (1987). "Musings: Teachers and the process of research." *Research in the Teaching of English.* 21, 5–7.

Atwell, N. (1982). "Class-based writing research: Teachers learn from students." *English Journal.* 71(1), 84–87.

———. (1986). "A more principled practice: The teacher researcher." Paper presented at New Directions in Composition Scholarship Conference, University of New Hampshire, Durham, N.H.

———. (1989). "The thoughtful practitioner." *Teachers Networking: The Whole Language Newsletter.* 9(3), 1, 10–12.

Berthoff, A. E. (1981). *The making of meaning.* Upper Montclair, N.J.: Boynton/Cook.

Bissex, G. L. (1988). "On learning and not learning from teaching." *Language Arts.* 65, 771–775.

Boomer, G. (1985). *Fair dinkum teaching and learning: Reflections on literacy and power.* Upper Montclair, N.J.: Boynton/Cook.

Britton, J. (1983). "A quiet form of research." *English Journal.* 72(4), 89–92.

Buckley, R. (1988). "From questions to new questions: Reflections." *Language Arts.* 65, 640–641.

Burton, F. R. (1988). "Reflections on Strickland's 'Toward the extended professional.'" *Language Arts.* 65, 765–768.

Calkins, L. M. (1985). "Forming research communities among naturalistic researchers," in B. W. McClelland and T. R. Donovan, eds. *Perspectives on research and scholarship in composition.* N.Y.: Modern Language Association, 125–144.

Casbergue, R. (1989). "The teacher as researcher." *Reading: Exploration and Discovery.* 11(2), 54–57.

Clark, C., and J. Elmore. (1981). "Transforming curriculum in mathematics, science, and writing: A case study of teacher yearly planning." Research series No. 99. East Lansing, MI.: Institute for Research on Teaching, Michigan State University.

Comber, B. (1988). "The continuing conversation: Choices in educational research." *Language Arts.* 65, 776–786.

Goswami, D. (1984). "Teachers as researchers," in R. Graves, ed. *Rhetoric and composition: A sourcebook for teachers and writers,* new edition. Upper Montclair, N.J.: Boynton/Cook, 347–358.

———, and P. R. Stillman. (1987). "Preface," in D. Goswami and P. Stillman, eds. *Reclaiming the classroom: Teacher research as an agency for change.* Upper Montclair, N.J.: Boynton/Cook.

Lee, S. C., R. Loven, and J. C. Stansell. (1988). "Process writing workshops: A move to teacher research." Paper presented at the fifth annual meeting of the National Reading and Language Arts Educators' Conference, Kansas City, MO.

McConaghy, J. (1986). "On becoming teacher experts: Research as a way of knowing." *Language Arts.* 63, 724–728.

Mohr, M. M. (1985). "What happened in their teaching? Appendix A," in M. Myers. *The teacher researcher: How to study writing in the classroom.* Urbana, IL.: National Council of Teachers of English, 127–129.

———. (1987). "Teacher researchers and the study of the writing process," in D. Goswami and P. Stillman, eds. *Reclaiming the classroom: Teacher research as an agency for change.* Upper Montclair, N.J.: Boynton/Cook, 94–106.

———, and M. Maclean. (1987). *Working together: A guide for teacher researchers.* Urbana, IL.: National Council of Teachers of English.

Myers, M. (1985). *The teacher researcher: How to study writing in the classroom.* Urbana, IL.: National Council of Teachers of English.

Patterson, L. A., and J. C. Stansell. (1987). "Teachers and researchers: A new mutualism." *Language Arts.* 64, 717–721.

Queenan, M. (1988). "Impertinent questions about teacher research: A review." *English Journal.* 77(2), 41–46.

Ray, L. C. (1987). "Reflections on classroom research," in D. Goswami and P. Stillman, eds. *Reclaiming the classroom: Teacher research as an agency for change.* Upper Montclair, N.J.: Boynton/Cook, 219–242.

Simmons, J., and G. Sparks. (1985). "Using research to develop professional thinking about teaching." *Journal of Staff Development.* 6, 106–115.

Strickland, D. S. (1988). "The teacher as researcher: Toward the extended professional." *Language Arts.* 65, 754–764.

———. (1988). "Reflections on Burton's reflections." *Language Arts.* 65, 769–770.

Warawa, B. (1988). "Classroom Inquiry: Learning about learning." *English Journal.* 77(2), 30–33.

Classroom Researchers as Theory Builders

Clark, C., and R. Yinger. (1977). "Research on teacher thinking." *Curriculum Inquiry.* 7, 279–304.

———. (1979). "Three studies of teacher planning." Research series No. 55. East Lansing, MI.: Institute for Research on Teaching, Michigan State University.

DeFord, D. E. (1979). "A validation study of an instrument to determine a teacher's theoretical orientation to reading instruction." Doctoral dissertation, Indiana University, Bloomington, IN.

———. (1985). "Validating the construct of theoretical orientation in reading instruction." *Reading Research Quarterly.* 20, 351–367.

Duffy, G. (1981). "Response to Borko, Shavelson, and Stern: There's more to instructional decision-making in reading than the 'empty classroom.'" *Reading Research Quarterly.* 17, 255–300.

———. (1982). "Fighting off the alligators: What research in real classrooms has to say about reading instruction." *Journal of Reading Behavior.* 14, 357–379.

———, and L. McIntyre. (1980). "A qualitative analysis of how various primary grade teachers employ the structured learning component of the direct instruction model when teaching reading." Research series No. 80. East Lansing, MI.: Institute for Research on Teaching, Michigan State University.

Harste, J. C., and C. L. Burke. (1977). "A new hypothesis for reading teacher education research: Both the teaching and the learning of reading are theoretically based," in P. D. Pearson, ed. *Reading: Research, theory, and practice: Twenty-sixth Yearbook of the National Reading Conference.* Clemson, S.C.: National Reading Conference, 32–40.

Kinzer, C., and D. Carrick. (1986). "Teacher beliefs as instructional influences," in J. Niles and R. Lalik, eds. *Solving problems in literacy: Learners, teachers, and researchers, thirty-fifth Yearbook of the National Reading Conference.* Rochester, N.Y.: National Reading Conference, 127–134.

Koech, B. (1983). "An investigation of factors influencing first grade teachers' selection and use of diagnostic procedures in beginning reading." Doctoral dissertation, University of Massachusetts, Amherst, MA.

Lee, S. C. (1987). "Teachers' perceptions of the process and function of theories of language learning." Doctoral dissertation, Texas A & M University, College Station, TX.

———. (1987). "Transactional theory: Not static, but dynamic." Paper presented at the thirty-seventh annual meeting of the National Reading Conference, St. Petersburg, FL.

———, and L. A. Patterson. (1988). "The nature of transactional theory: Not static, but dynamic." Unpublished paper.

Mitchell, K. (1980). "Patterns of teacher-student responses to oral reading errors as related to teachers' theoretical frameworks." *Research in the Teaching of English. 14,* 243–263.

Shake, M. (1984). "The congruence between instructional philosophies and practices: A study of teacher thinking." Doctoral dissertation, State University of New York at Albany, N.Y.

Stansell, J. C., and L. A. Patterson. (1987). "Beyond teacher research: The teacher as theory builder." Paper presented at the thirty-seventh annual meeting of the National Reading Conference, St. Petersburg, FL.

Naturalistic Classroom Research: Theory and Practice

Bouffler, C. (1984). "A case study exploration of functional strategies in spelling." Doctoral dissertation, Indiana University, Bloomington, IN.

Clay, M. (1982). "Looking and seeing in the classroom." *English Journal. 71*(2), 80–92.

Dewey, J., and A. F. Bentley. (1949). *Knowing and the known.* Boston, MA.: Beacon.

Donaldson, M. (1978). *Children's minds.* Glasgow: William Collins.

Green, J., and D. Bloome. (1983). "Ethnography and reading: Issues, approaches, criteria, and findings," in J. Niles and L. Harris, eds. *Searches for meaning in reading/language processing and instruction.* Thirty-second Yearbook of the National Reading Conference. Rochester, N.Y.: National Reading Conference, 6–30.

Halliday, M. A. K., and R. Hasan. (1980). *Text and context: A social-semiotic perspective.* Tokyo, Japan: Sophia University Press.

Harste, J. C. (1985). "Portrait of a new paradigm: Reading comprehension research," in A. Crismore, ed. *Landscapes: A state-of-the-art assessment of reading comprehension research.* Final report, Project USDE-C-300-83-0130. Bloomington, IN.: Language Education Departments, Indiana University.

———, V. A. Woodward, and C. L. Burke. (1984). *Language stories and literacy lessons.* Portsmouth, N.H.: Heinemann.

Heath, S. B. (1983). *Ways with words: Language, life, and work in communities and schools.* Cambridge, G.B.: Cambridge University Press.

Herzfeld, H. (1981). "Signs in the field: Prospects and issues for semiotic ethnography." *Semiotics. 46,* 99–106.

Lightfoot, S. L. (1983). *The good high school.* N.Y.: Basic.

Lincoln, Y., and E. Guba. (1985). *Naturalistic inquiry.* Beverly Hills, CA.: Sage.

Patterson, L. A. (1987). "Transactional research: Not a methodology, but a stance." Paper presented at the thirty-seventh annual meeting of the National Reading Conference, St. Petersburg, FL.

Rogers, V. (1984). "Qualitative research: Another way of knowing," in P. Hosford, ed. *Using what we know about teaching.* Alexandria, VA.: Association for Supervision and Curriculum Development.

Rosenblatt, L. M. (1978). *The reader, the text, the poem: The transactional theory of the literary work.* Carbondale, IL.: Southern Illinois University Press.

———. (1985). "Transaction versus interaction: A terminological rescue operation." *Research in the Teaching of English. 19,* 96–107.

Shanklin, N. C. (1982). *Relating reading and writing: Developing a transactional theory of the writing process.* Monographs in Language and Reading Series, No. 3. Bloomington, IN.: Indiana University School of Education.

Stenhouse, L. (1975). *An introduction to curriculum research and development.* London: Heinemann.

———. (1981). "What counts as research?" *British Journal of Educational Studies. 29,* 103–114.

———. (1985). "Action research and the teacher's responsibility for the educational process," in J. Rudduck and D. Hopkins, eds. *Research as a basis for teaching: Readings from the work of Lawrence Stenhouse.* London: Heinemann, 56–58.

Appendix B. Examples of Ways to Record Data

Data-gathering in a naturalistic study must be systematic and must leave a "paper trail" that can document the research process. These forms are examples of ways in which teachers have recorded data in classrooms at various grade levels. Consider these as examples only; the particular form a teacher decides to use depends on the research focus and the particular research questions. Refer to the bibliography in Appendix A for books that offer more comprehensive and detailed suggestions for methodological procedures.

EARLY CHILDHOOD OR KINDERGARTEN CLASSROOMS

Each of these forms will yield the same kind of information. The checklist may be more helpful for those who are beginning to observe children; whereas the anecdotal log may be more helpful for those who want a more flexible procedure. Once a decision is made about what will be observed (the following list is merely an example), it is easy to modify the categories.

The open-ended observation sheet allows the teacher to document any student behavior that is felt to be important in learning more about students' communication patterns. For example, after data is collected over a period of weeks the teacher might choose to drop the category concerning family events and focus on messages specifically regarding books. In this way the data-gathering process helps to define and limit the focus of the study.

Communication Patterns: Checklist

Name	Uses a picture book to tell a story	Tells a story about a family event	Asks question during shared reading	Talks to a friend about a book	Brings a book from home to share

Communication Patterns: Anecdotal Log

Child's Name	Date	Observation

EARLY ELEMENTARY CLASSROOMS

Independent Reading Form

Name: _____   Observation Period: _____

	Selected	Finished
1. Books read during sustained silent reading time (SSR)		
2. Books checked out of school library		
3. Books brought from home		
4. Books checked out of classroom library		

When the student reads:

Date	SSR	Free choice time	Home	After work is done	Other	Comments

MIDDLE SCHOOL

The teacher who is using a writing workshop in a middle-school language arts class would certainly have much more data available than is shown in the following chart. The teacher would know the number of pieces published, the topics, the length, accuracy in writing conventions, and much more. The teacher who developed the checklist was concerned that her students were not fully using revision opportunities. As an instructional tool this checklist helped her see which students needed more support during the revision process. As a research tool the checklist answered her questions about who was revising and which classroom routines were more consistently used.

Writing Process Checklist

Name	Made change in first draft	Read draft to peer	Took draft to author's circle	Abandoned piece	Made changes after author's circle	Editor's table	Recopied piece/ published

Appendix C. Roots of Teacher Research: A Chronology

Katherine P. McFarland

Aristotle (4th century B.C.)	Emphasized the role of observation.
Comenius (late 1640s)	Wrote *Pampaedia,* a treatise on child observation and teaching methods.
Rousseau (1762)	Wrote *Emile,* a fictional work on observing nature in relation to the child.
Pestalozzi (late 18th century)	Encouraged inquiry methods of observation to meet disadvantaged students' needs.
Francis W. Parker (1880s)	Encouraged teachers in his Cook County (IL.) school to observe children; around 1900 their studies began to be published in *The Elementary School Teacher and the Course of Study,* a monograph series.
John Dewey (1890s)	Put his educational theories, based on observation of students, into practice in his lab school in Chicago.
Maria Montessori (1907)	Began training teachers to use observation and experimentation in her schools in Italy.
Lucy Sprague Mitchell (1916)	Founded the Bureau of Educational Experiments, which supported and published teachers' studies of children, their nature, and their growth. BEE later became the Bank Street College of Education.

Kurt Lewin
(1946)

Coined the term "action research" to describe qualitative studies aimed at solving social problems arising during and after World War II.

Stephen M. Corey
(early 1950s)

With colleagues at Teachers College, Columbia University, facilitated studies by teachers across the country through the Horace Mann-Lincoln Institute of School Experimentation.

Lawrence Stenhouse
(1970s)

Supported and collaborated with British teacher researchers through the Center for Applied Research in Education, University of East Anglia. His associate, John Elliott, founded the Cambridge Institute of Education, a network for teacher researchers, in 1974.

Collaboratives that involve teacher researchers
(founded 1970s–1980s)

1976: Institute for Research on Teaching, Michigan State University.

1987: Texas A & M School/University Research Collaborative's Teacher as Researcher Project.

Appendix D. Education Associations that Disseminate Information through Conferences and/or Journals

American Educational Research Association, 1230 17th Street, NW, Washington, DC 20036

American Psychological Association, 1400 North Uhle St., Arlington, VA 22201

Association for Supervision and Curriculum Development, 225 N. Washington St., Alexandria, VA 22314

Indiana Teachers of Writing, Indiana University-Purdue University at Indianapolis, 425 Agnes St., Indianapolis, IN 46202

International Council for Computers in Education, University of Oregon, 1787 Agate St., Eugene, OR 87403

International Reading Association, 800 Barksdale Rd., PO Box 8139, Newark, DE 19711

Linguistic Society of America, 3520 Prospect St., NW, Washington, DC 20007

National Art Education Association, 1916 Association Dr., Reston, VA 22091

National Association for Biology Teachers, 1120 Roger Bacon Dr., Reston, VA 22090

National Association for the Education of Young Children, 1834 Connecticut Ave., NW, Washington, DC 20009

National Council of Teachers of English, 1111 Kenyon Rd., Urbana, IL 61801

National Council of Teachers of Mathematics, 1906 Association Dr., Reston, VA 22091

National Science Teachers Association, 1742 Connecticut Ave., NW, Washington, DC 20009

Ontario Modern Language Teachers Association, 4 Oakmount Rd., Welland, ON L3C 4X8, Canada

Pi Lambda Theta, 4101 E. 3rd St., Bloomington, IN 47401

School Science and Mathematics Association, 126 Life Science Building, Bowling Green State University, Bowling Green, OH 43403–0256

Teachers and Writers Collaborative, 5 Union Square West, New York, NY 10003

Appendix E. Example of a Proposal Accepted for Presentation at the Annual Convention of the International Reading Association

Title

Great Beginnings: Supporting Children's Literacy Growth through the Primary Grades

Grade Levels

Pre-K through grade 3

Intended Audience

Classroom teachers, Chapter I teachers, reading specialists, parents

Objectives of the Program

The primary goal of this microworkshop is to present both the rationale and techniques for providing children with a positive start toward becoming effective life-long readers. Through small-group activities the audience will explore:

1. strategies for developing reading/writing skills;
2. new uses for predictable books, big books, and posters;

3. story-telling as a language activity;
4. read-aloud techniques with follow-up strategies;
5. state-level assessment of language learning.

Content to Be Presented

The small-group sessions will invite the audience to explore activities to encourage language learning in the classroom and the assessment of language at the state level. Four small-group sessions will involve the audience in the demonstration of language-learning activities appropriate for preschool/primary grades based on the newest research in language learning. A fifth small-group session will explore what can be learned through state-level assessment. Specifically, the content for each objective is as follows:

1. Reading/Writing Skills
   demonstrations of the use of children's literature, language experience connections, and shared book experiences, etc.
2. Predictable/Pattern Books
   effective uses of predictable and patterned books, big books, and posters with a slotting technique, as well as other new activities
3. Story-telling
   the use of story-telling to involve children in reading, writing, creative dramatics, and other language activities
4. Reading Aloud
   how, why, and what to read aloud to sell the love of reading in the classroom
5. State-level Assessment
   the interaction between state assessment and whole language programs with implications for classroom assessment and instruction.

Methods of Presenting Content

The proposed microworkshop will provide the audience with an opportunity to participate as much as possible. The workshop will begin with a brief welcome, an opening statement, introduction of staff members, and description of the format of the workshop. Members of the audience will select the sessions of most interest to them from descriptions of the microworkshop program, and attend three of the five repeated small-group sessions. The microworkshop will conclude with brief closing remarks on future directions of literacy learning.

The timetable for the microworkshop will be as follows:

Time/Min	Activity
15	Opening remarks
5	Selection of first session

40	Session 1
5	Selection of second session
40	Session 2
5	Selection of third session
40	Session 3
15	Closing remarks, questions

Methods of presenting content in the various sessions will include the following:

introduction of content through discussion/visual aids
displays of materials
audience participation in activities
handouts of additional ideas not presented
bibliographies of professional books on the topic
bibliographies of children's literature
bibliographies of appropriate educational materials
question/answer sessions

Name Index

Subject Index

About the Authors

Leslie Patterson is assistant professor in the Division of Teacher Education at Sam Houston State University in Huntsville, Texas. For nine years prior to that she taught junior high and high school language arts in both rural and suburban schools. The classroom research project she began in 1983 (*see* Chapter 3) led her to conduct other research, to write for publication, and to participate in a wide range of professional activities. As a university teacher researcher she now attempts to engage her students as kidwatchers and theory builders within the context of graduate and undergraduate courses in reading/language arts. She is a member of Center for Expansion of Language and Thinking, the National Council of Teachers of English, the International Reading Association, IRA's Teaching as a Researching Profession Special Interest Group, and IRA's Teacher as Researcher Committee.

John C. Stansell is a university-based teacher researcher at Texas A&M University. As a Professor in the Department of Educational Curriculum and Instruction he teaches reading/language arts courses that involve both practicing and preservice teachers in doing research. He also teaches a graduate course on naturalistic research and one on teacher research. During the last thirteen years he has been studying his own classes to learn more about the development of teachers' theories of language learning and how to encourage that development, helping teachers study their students and their teaching, working with doctoral students whose dissertations involved research in their classrooms, and writing articles and conference papers about these experiences. He now serves as Coordinator of The Teacher as Researcher Project of the Texas A&M School/University Research Collaborative, which helped support more than twenty studies by teachers in ten Texas school districts in the last two years. He is an active member of Center for Expansion of Language and Thinking, the National Council of Teachers of English, and the International Reading Association, and a charter member of the IRA's Teaching as a Researching Profession Special Interest Group.

Sharon Lee is currently a teacher researcher at the University of South Dakota. She teachers graduate and undergraduate courses in reading/language arts and has a strong interest in middle school education. She brings to that current work both her experience as a middle level reading and English teacher and her interest in the development of teachers' personal theories and instructional decision making. She is participating in a number of staff development projects in local school districts. She is a member of the Center for the Expansion of Language and Thinking, the National Council of Teachers of English, International Reading Association, and a charter member of IRA's Teaching as a Researching Profession Special Interest Group. She is also a state officer of the South Dakota Reading Council and an active member of the National Middle School Association.

Terresa Payne Katt is currently the Elementary Coordinator for the Spring Branch Independent School District in Houston, Texas. After earning her degree at Texas A&M University Terresa began her classroom career at Wilchester Elementary School in Texas, initially as a third-grade teacher, after which she moved to the first grade and then to prekindergarten.

R. Kay Moss is Associate Professor in Specialized Development at Illinois State University. With a doctorate from Texas A&M University, the author has experience as both a university professor and as a Reading Teacher and Reading Specialist in the Middle School. Author of a large number of journal articles, Dr. Moss was Editor for *Reading: Exploration and Discovery* and is on the Editorial Advisory Board for *Reading Teacher*.